C000117826

Discover North Norfolk

Maps. Ordnance Survey maps 132, 133 and 134 of the Landranger series cover north Norfolk at a scale of 1:50,000, approximately 1.25 inches to 1 mile.

Notes for foreign readers. Before **decimalisation** in 1971, British currency had 12 pennies or pence to a shilling, and 20 shillings to a pound. Six shillings and eightpence was written either 6s 8d or 6/8d and was worth 33p in decimal terms. **B&B** means 'bed and breakfast,' usually available in private houses, farmhouses or pubs (public houses). You will see the sign all over the country and in this book. American readers should note that their 'first floor' is the British **ground floor,** their second the British first.

Cover: Cley mill

Discover
North
Norfolk

Terry Palmer

**HERITAGE
HOUSE**

DISCOVER NORTH NORFOLK

First published April 1992
Second edition, revised, May 1995

ISBN 1.85215.1161
Printed in Hong Kong. Published by Heritage House (Publishers) Ltd,
Steam Mill Road, Bradfield, Manningtree, CO11 2QT

© **Terry Palmer, 1992, 1995.**
The right of Terry Palmer to be identified as author of this work has
been asserted by him in accordance with the Copyright, Design and
Patents Act, 1988.

All rights reserved. No part of this publication may be reproduced, stored in a
retrieval system, or transmitted in any form whatever, except for brief extracts for
reviews, without the written permission of the publisher.

Acknowledgements. Michael Barrett, Gresham School; David Case, Wells Harbour
Commissioners; Denis Condon, Worstead; Lt Cmdr Francis, Wells & Walsingham
Railway; Frances Hoyo, South Gate, King's Lynn; Jim Jordan, Swaffham; Lorraine
Marshall and Graham Walker, Wells Harbourmaster's Office; Mark Regan,
Whitechapel Bell Foundry, London; Dr Wells, Heacham; Les Winter, Burnham
Thorpe.

Other titles on East Anglia. *Discover The Lower Stour, Discover The Suffolk Coast, A
Day Out In Southwold.*

CONTENTS

MAPS

The ford at Glandford: motorists beware!

1: STEP BACK IN TIME

A Norfolk overview – with railway history

NORFOLK IS A FASCINATING COUNTY. One of the driest parts of Britain, it has Broadland to the east, Fenland to the west, and the dry sands of Breckland on its southern flank.

It is among the lowest counties in Britain – the highest point is Brink Hill near Great Massingham, at 305ft (93m) above sea level – but it certainly is not flat. A ridge of chalk, topped locally with **carrstone**, a sandstone with a high iron content, runs from Hunstanton's colourful cliffs down to Newmarket Heath; the chalk eventually becomes the Chiltern Hills. East of the carrstone strip the optimistically-named 'High Norfolk' has fair grade farmland brought down from the north during the Ice Ages. Ice? The hills behind Cromer and Sheringham are **terminal moraines**, the final dumping-ground of the glaciers before they retreated.

Coast and Country. North Norfolk has a beautiful, unspoiled coastline. The main road is still a country lane, and pressures of city life are forgotten. In summer the fields are green with sugar beet, gold with ripening wheat, pastel blue with linseed (flax) and yellow with oilseed rape, which is ousting the traditional mustard for Colman's of Norwich. You can still find sheep on the rougher land and cattle on the marshes, but East Anglia has long ceased to produce wool by the cartload as it did in the Middle Ages - although the village of **Worsted** is a living reminder of the worstead once woven there.

But in midwinter it can be bleak, when an icy wind scythes down from the Arctic. There is no land between this coast and the North Pole, and beyond that lies Siberia.

Norfolk worthies. The county has strong Royal connections, particularly at **Sandringham** and at nearby King's Lynn, while in the east, **Blickling** was the home of **Anne Boleyn**. Norfolk also gave us **Robert Walpole**, who created the job of Prime Minister; **Thomas Edward Coke** and **'Turnip' Townshend** who both revolutionised farming; and **Horatio Nelson** who became one of the country's greatest admirals.

Norfolk, indeed, has always been a maritime county, although the sea has treated it harshly. You can draw a map of the coast from Weybourne to Great Yarmouth with a single sweep of the pen, the mark of erosive tides for ever sweeping south-east along the shore. Yet to the west of Weybourne the water is in retreat as **Blakeney Point** and **Scolt Head** continue to grow, and **The Wash** silts up.

CHURCHES

For many visitors, Norfolk is a county of churches, each one the focal point of a bustling village in the days of the wool trade when Norfolk had the densest rural population in England. The dying cloth industry killed many villages, but their churches remain; although most are medieval they usually stand on established sites. Indeed, 119 of them have **round towers**, a mark of their Saxon origins although a few were built in Norman times. There are 41 round towers in Suffolk and only 14 elsewhere in Britain.

Why round? Because you cannot build square corners in flint; you need stone or brick, which the Saxons did not have. Only after the Norman Conquest were cornerstones shipped in from Normandy – it was more convenient that hauling them from Leicestershire – and round towers were no longer built.

Know your church. The **tower** evolved as a place to hang the bell, which summoned people to prayer, but towers were also refuges against marauders, landmarks for fishermen and even storehouses for grain, safe from rats. It is difficult to find anywhere in Norfolk that is out of sight of a church tower, and from several high spots you can see at least half a dozen.

The **nave** is the main part of the building, its roof often looking like an upturned boat, hence the *naval* link. It is invariably built east-west and almost always with the tower at the western end; on rare occasions the tower is offset or freestanding. Most churches have a **chapel** at the east end of the nave; before the 16th-cent reformation when Henry VIII became a 'protestant' against Catholicism, the priest was responsible for building and maintaining the chapel, and he usually had his own private door into it. The churchwardens were responsible for the rest of the building.

Between nave and chapel was the **rood beam**, a sturdy timber 10ft to 15ft (3m to 5m) up, carrying the **rood screen**. The **rood** itself was the carving of the crucified Christ and the subject of medieval oaths when people swore 'by the rood.' No church kept its rood after the Reformation, but a few still have traces of the rood stair set into the outer wall.

It was normal practise to enter the church through the **south porch**, on the sunny side, while the door in the **north porch** was left open during baptisms for the Devil to escape. Modern road systems sometimes make the north porch more convenient, but of the county's 660 churches, 468 use the south door, 152 the north, while 40 have a west door, usually through the tower.

The **east window** is the main source of light above the high altar and often has the best stained glass.

Even **tombs** have their messages in code. A man with crossed arms or legs had been on a Crusade to the Holy Land, but a person whose feet rested on a little dog had died peacefully in bed.

One of the surviving fords in Norfolk – but it's useful for cleaning all makes of car.

Yew trees had been planted in English churchyards since the coming of Christianity, but we are only now learning their symbolism, and a 1,200-year-old yew can pinpoint the site of a Saxon church even if no other trace remains.

RAILWAYS

Norfolk had a good rail network on nationalisation in 1948, but economies and line closures have hit the county badly. The **Great Eastern** ran from Liverpool Street to King's Lynn and Hunstanton, with a branch line from Lynn to Swaffham, Dereham, Wymondham and Norwich, and another from Heacham to Wells, Fakenham and Dereham. There was a further loop from Dereham to North Elmham and Aylsham to Wroxham, where it met the Norwich to Cromer line. Another line joined Norwich and Yarmouth Vauxhall, via Acle.

The **Midland and Great Northern Joint Railway**, the old M&GN, the 'muddle and get nowhere,' ran from Wisbech North to Lynn, then on to Fakenham, Melton Constable, Aylsham and Yarmouth Beach; there were branch lines to Norwich, and to Holt, Sheringham and Cromer; a tiny stretch of this survives as the **North Norfolk Railway**, the 'Poppy Line.'

Lynn & Dereham. The Lynn & Dereham Line, incorporated in 1845 with £270,000 capital, was a continuation of the Lynn & Ely, and the two soon became the **East Anglian Railway**. The double-track line to Narborough opened on 27 October 1846 and reached Swaffham on 10 August 1847. It struggled on to Sporle by 26 October and entered Dereham on 11 September 1848.

The L&D had major problems: the high cost of land and cutting through the chalk at Swaffham raised the cost to £24,000 a mile, and bankrupted the contractors.

By 1897 it was running eight services daily, which rose to nine in 1914 and peaked at 12 in 1955 as a branch of British Railways. From 1900 it took coaches from Doncaster to Yarmouth, and from 1916 added coaches from York.

In 1961 the service was down to nine local diesel cars daily; in April 1966 most freight traffic stopped; in August all stations were unmanned, and on 9 September 1968 the line closed. Its revenue was then £22,000 a year, with costs at £46,000.

The **Norfolk Railway** carved a track from Norwich through Wymondham to Dereham. Authorised in 1845 it hauled freight from 7 December 1846 and passengers from 15 February 1847.

The Dereham to Wells and Blakeney extension got no further than Fakenham, opening on 20 March 1849. The **Wells & Fakenham Railway** finished it; incorporated in 1854, it had £10,000 capital from the Earl of Leicester, owner of Holkham Hall; £14,000 from the town of Wells; and £30,000 from the directors of the Norfolk Railway. The line opened on 1 December 1857, which was declared a public holiday, with the Wells Harbour extension coming in 1859.

Then in 1862 the GER absorbed the W&FR, and 30 years later Wells had a daily through coach to Liverpool St. Silting of the harbour reduced goods traffic, but day trippers came in their thousands from Norwich, and the line brought many pilgrims to Walsingham.

In decline, the Wells to Heacham line was a victim of the East Coast floods of January 1953, and the last passenger on the W&FR travelled on 5 October 1964. Freight traffic ceased at the month's end, and by January 1983 the line stopped at North Elmham; this spur closed six years later.

The **Lynn & Fakenham Railway** opened its Gaywood to Massingham track on 16 August 1879, and extended it to Fakenham a year later, to the day, using three locos from the Cornish Railway. The M&GN bought the line in 1893 and did reasonable business with farm produce, but passenger traffic was never profitable. The line was at its busiest in the 1930s and carried 571 trainloads of aviation fuel to RAF bases in World War Two. Traffic declined when peace came, and the last passenger travelled on 2 March 1959, the last freight on 1 May 1968.

Thelmethorpe Curve. The GER's Wroxham to Dereham line ran parallel with the M&GN's Cromer to Norwich line for a mile, near the village of Thelmethorpe, after the former went under a bridge carrying the latter. When both lines were facing closure, British Rail abandoned the bridge and joined the lines with the Thelmethorpe Curve, 518yds (472m) of track that opened on 12 September 1960 – but closed to passengers in February 1969 and to goods in January 1982.

Lynn & Hunstanton. The single-track Lynn & Hunstanton Railway opened on 3 October 1862, the year that the Prince of Wales bought Sandringham House. Hunstanton had fewer than 500 people in the 1861 census, but had more than 1,000 a decade later as it became fashionable. Snettisham's fishermen sent their catch by rail, joining the grain, cattle, manure and coal to form the bulk of the freight traffic.

Hunstanton's L'Estrange family gave most of the ground needed for the line, which was therefore built for less than £60,000. The GER operated the line for half the takings, plus £10 per track mile per week – but the L&HR had to pay compensation when the train hit a bull in August 1863. Seven people were killed, as well as the bull.

In 1874 the L&HR merged with the **West Norfolk Junction Railway** and the two were swallowed by the GER on 1 July 1890. The GER doubled the track from Lynn to Wolferton by 1899, in view of the Royal traffic, with the Prince of Wales paying for Wolferton Station.

By 1900 there were 12 trains daily each way in summer, six in winter, with connections to Liverpool St in 187 minutes and to St Pancras in 184. In 1905 a restaurant car was added on golfers' request.

The railways had started a major social revolution in rural Britain, with East Anglia's scattered population benefiting most: never before had so many people been able to afford the luxury of travel. In 1922 there were 14 summer trains daily each way, with extras on Sundays.

Traffic was severely reduced in World War Two, but in the late 1940s summer excursion trains to Hunstanton were packed; nobody minded standing. Fifteen years later the traffic was on the roads, with homeward traffic queueing from Sandringham to get through the bottleneck of King's Lynn. In those days even traffic jams were a novelty.

St. George and the dragon at Cley.

Drama in the Floods. There was drama on this line in the East Coast Floods of 1953. On 31 January the 1927 down train was caught in the high tide north of Heacham; a floating bungalow hit the smoke stack, damaged the vacuum brakes, and put the fire out. The train was stuck for six hours, with the floodwaters reaching seat level. As the tide receded the footplate crew used the tender floor as fuel and crawled back to Hunstanton. So many beach huts had been washed onto the line that it was blocked until 23 February.

The line was already dying. Diesel cars replaced steam in 1958, and on summer Sundays in 1966 there were just two excursions to Hunstanton from Liverpool St, and they ceased forever at the season's end.

From 1967 stations were unmanned, and there was one platform in use at Hunstanton. Level crossing gates were replaced by the first automatic barriers in Britain, and all signalling was controlled from Lynn. BR cut the running costs from £100,000 a year to £35,000, but the income of £40,000 also slumped. The line closed on 5 May 1969.

Heacham to Wells. The West Norfolk Junction Railway opened the Heacham to Wells line on 17 August 1866, but the Prince and Princess of Wales had a privilege trip to Holkham on 13 January. The GER operated the line on a partnership, and took it over on 1 July 1890. Its passenger service was an early victim, closing on 2 June 1952. The floods of early 1953 damaged the Burnham Market to Wells section, and forced its closure to passengers; freight traffic to Heacham survived until 28 December 1964.

East Norfolk Railway. The East Norfolk Railway, incorporated in 1864, began work on the Whitlingham Junction (Norwich) to North Walsham line in 1865 but stopped when the contractor died and his assets were frozen. Work resumed in 1870, and in 1872 the ENR had Parliamentary approval to extend the track to Cromer – but Cromer didn't want it.

A single track opened to North Walsham on 20 October 1874, to Gunton on 29 July 1876 and, despite the objections, to Cromer on 26 March 1877.

The GER took control in 1881, and between 1896 and 1900 doubled the track to Walsham. The first train from London took 310 minutes to Cromer, but on 1 July 1897 the daily *Cromer Express* did the journey, non-stop to Walsham, in 175 minutes. Renamed the *Norfolk Coast Express* with 12 coaches, this was the pride of the GER until the First World War. After the Second War the *Norfolkman* and *Broadsman* revived the tradition for a few years.

Then on 18 June 1985 the Post Office chartered the *Orient Express* to come to Cromer. The journey was possible only because the only town that didn't want the railway is, with Sheringham, the only one that still has it.

FOOTPATHS

Norfolk has fewer footpaths and bridleways than most rural counties, but it has a great network of country lanes, a relic of medieval times and the wool trade. The decline in population since then means that there are few cars on most of these byways.

Among the major paths are **Peddars Way**, from mid- Suffolk to Holme next the Sea near Hunstanton. The Romans built it in a straight line, but today's path has a few kinks and ranges from tarmac lanes to footpaths, and goes through only one village, **Castle Acre**.

At Holme it meets the **Norfolk Coast Path**, meandering from Hunstanton to Cromer along some splendid if undramatic scenery and past several nature reserves. At Cromer the **Weavers' Way** begins, taking walkers on a circuitous route inland to Great Yarmouth. And from Yarmouth the **Angles' Way**, also called the **Waveney Way**, leads back to Diss and follows the Little Ouse River until it meets the Peddars Way again.

NATURE RESERVES.

The Norfolk Wildlife Trust at 72 Cathedral Close, Norwich, NR1 4DF (01603 625540) has 14 reserves. Those in our area, with the RSPB's two, are:

Roydon Common, 3 miles NE of Lynn on A148 then signposted south. Sandy heath and wetlands; always open.

Narborough Railway Line, 1 mile S of Narborough, SE of Lynn; disused rail embankment has rich chalk-grassland flora & fauna, especially butterflies; always open.

Snettisham, RSPB reserve with hides. Common tern; duck. Always open; signed from Snettisham.

Holme Dunes, north of A149 at Holme; saltmarsh, dune, wetland; excellent during migrations with 280 species recorded. Open daily, 1000-1700; fee.

Titchwell Marsh, RSPB reserve with hides; ringed plover, ruff, dunlin, black tern, some kingfisher. At low tide, remains of **petrified forest** visible. Shop, WC, picnic site.

Scolt Head Island – see chapter 3.

Cley Marshes, major site, more than 300 bird species seen. Hides. Tues-Sun, Apr-Oct 1000-1700; fee.

Foxley Wood, 2 miles N of Bawdeswell, near Thelmethorpe Curve. Britain's largest stand of ancient woodland; butterflies & flowers. Open year round Fri-Wed 1000-1700.

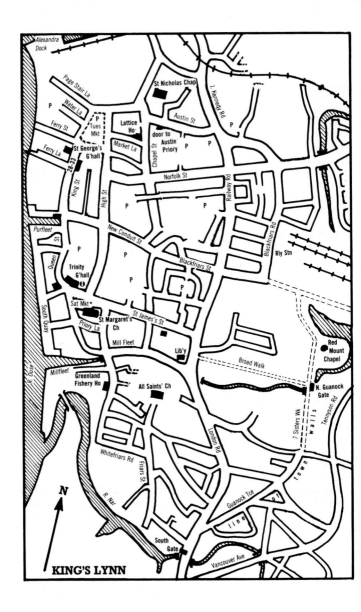

KING'S LYNN

2: KING'S LYNN

Royal Norfolk

BEFORE 1537, KING'S LYNN was called 'Bishop's Lynn.' The bishop in question was Herbert de Losinga who in 1094 paid William II some 1,000 marks (£666) for the office and title of Bishop of Norwich.

When Norwich Cathedral was consecrated in 1101, Pope Paschal II learned of the bribe and ordered Bishop de Losinga to build churches and priories as penance. Among them were **Holy Mary Magdalene and St Margaret and All Holy Virgins**. Now known as St Margaret's, it was built on saltmarsh that the bishop owned in the settlement called Linn, from the Saxon word for a small lake. Linn took the name of 'Bishop Losinga' later changing it to 'Bishop's Lynn,' with its new Saturday Market beside St Margaret's Church.

Bishop Turbe of Norwich (1146–74) was not to be outsmarted by Losinga so he built his own town a mile to the north, gave it the Church of St Nicholas and another market, to be held on Tuesday.

Two towns. So there were two towns – until John granted the Royal Charter in 1204 and so united them. Medieval markets could not survive without royal approval and John allowed both to thrive, which is why Lynn still has two markets to this day.

Turbe's town was designed on the grid system with all plots commanding equal rents, as is recorded on a 13th-cent plan still surviving. When the system was compiled, Turbe's part of town was the more popular so almost all the plots were taken, and the black-robed Augustinian friars, reorganised in the 12th cent, were lucky to find a site near Tuesday Market; their friary is remembered in the name Austin Street, where the doorway stands as a sole relic.

Other friars. The Dominicans, also known as Black Friars from their black hoods worn over white cloaks; the Fransiscans or Grey Friars; and the Carmelites or White Friars, all had to find plots in Losinga's Lynn. **Greyfriars Tower** in Tower Gardens near the library is the only part of the 15th-cent priory to survive the Dissolution of the Monasteries; an archway of the 12th-cent **Benedictine Priory** stands in Priory Lane, south of St Margaret's Church; while Blackfriars St near the museum, and Whitefriars Road near Friars Fleet mark the sites of the other orders.

The Benedictines of St Margaret's Church had rights over the income from the Saturday Market until Bishop John de Grey of Norwich took them over in 1205. The Carmelites were weird: they never spoke a word and they slept in their own coffins. The Austins had an altar called the 'Stairway to Heaven' in their church, and they sang mass over their dead. The Dominicans were burned out in 1486, when Lynn had more than 70 religious orders, but escaped the Dissolution and survived until 1845.

Massacre of the Jews. By contrast, Jews were barely tolerated. Many were massacred in Jews' Lane – now Surrey St – by Tuesday Market in 1189 to mark preparations for Richard I's departure on the Third Crusade. No trace of their homes remains.

●

The AFRICAN VIOLET CENTRE

This unique attraction was established in 1968 by the Reverend Tony Clements, and transferred to Terrington St Clement in the Fens in 1973. Since that time, under the continuing direction of its founder, popularly known as the Violets Vicar, it has developed into a major Norfolk attraction.

Chelsea Flowers. The nursery's main feature is its display of African violets, thousands of plants in all stages of growth and many hundreds of them in bloom. An exhibitor at the Chelsea Flower Show since 1979, Tony Clements has been awarded the Royal Horticultural Society's Gold Medal on at least six occasions since 1988.

African violets for exhibition are prepared in a private show glasshouse, but if you would like a peep, it's worth asking.

The new display glasshouse contains a stunning show of violets in bloom, and you may also visit the propagation house, the gift shop, and the tea room. There are toilets and ample parking, and disabled visitors are particularly welcome; there is wheelchair access everywhere.

Regular events include orchid shows, a cactus show, and a fuchsia weekend; details and dates are available by phone. The Violets Vicar's centre is beside the A17 five miles west of King's Lynn; open daily, Feb-Christmas, 1000-1700 – free. 01553.828374.

Picture shows a section of the display glasshouse. See also page24.

●

Fleet. 'Fleet' is an old word for 'shallow,' but in Lynn it means 'shallow river.' The **Millfleet** was bridged in 1250, linking Bishop's Lynn with the village of South Lynn, while the **Purfleet**, the original port, marked the rough boundary between the two Lynns, with **Fisher Fleet** the northern boundary.

And fleets. The town's location at the mouth of the Great Ouse,

HOLKHAM HALL TODAY

Holkham Hall is among England's most majestic of stately homes. Indeed, it is difficult to decide which is the more impressive, the lavish building or its sumptuous contents, which include many works by Gainsborough, Rubens, Van Dyck and others. The alabaster entrance hall is a masterpiece which sets the tone of what is to follow as you walk through room after room, seeing exquisite furniture, much of it by William Kent, and enormous tapestries. At one time the library grew so much that many books had to be moved to the Bodleian at Oxford, and the collection is still one of Britain's biggest.

The gardens. When Thomas Coke died, his widow the Countess of Leicester commissioned 'Capability' Brown to design the ornamental gardens. Brown was so much in demand that he made a great fortune, but the grounds at Holkham show he had great skill as well.

The Garden Centre. Today, the 6-acre (2.5ha) walled kitchen garden, still holding the orangery and vinery, grows roses, alpines, bedding plants and pot plants for sale; it is open year round, Mon-Sat, afternoons. 01328.710374.

Holkham Pottery. The estate opened Holkham Pottery in 1951 to make high quality souvenirs, and you can see the potters and painters at work, Mon-Fri, afternoons. 01328.710424.

Bygones. The vast collection of old household items that featured on Anglia Television's *Bygones* programmes is permanently housed in Holkham's converted stables. You can find steam engines and fire engines, motor bikes and milk churns, a smithy and a laundry, and much else besides. Other attractions include a gift shop, Easter-Oct, a display of the History of Farming, and a cruise on the park's lake in an electrically-powered launch.

Open. Holkham Hall itself is open Sun-Thur, May-Sep, afternoons. Basic admission fee to Hall *or* Bygones; higher rate covers everything. 01328.710227. *Picture: aerial view of Holkham Hall.* See also page 48.

●

sheltered yet prone to flooding, turned the people's minds to maritime trade. From earliest times, ships sailed across to the Low Countries and Saxony, bringing wealth; after the Great Fire of 1331 which destroyed most of the daub-and-wattle-and-thatch houses, the burghers found they could afford to rebuild with brick and tile, although these materials were more costly than Baltic softwood and Norfolk's own reeds.

GUILDHALLS

The **Guild of St George**, founded in 1376, met in the 13th-cent hall of the Holy Trinity where it received its charter from Henry IV in 1406. The hall had escaped the 1331 fire but the guildsmen, wanting their own base,

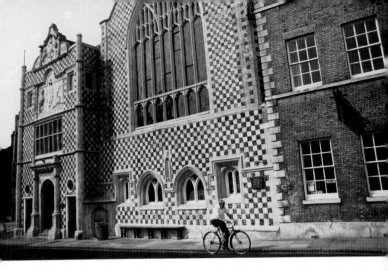

The Guild of Holy Trinity in King's Lynn is one of the oldest in England.

built it between 1410 and 1420 by Tuesday Market. It is an unassuming place but as WW2 bombing damaged the guildhalls of London and York, St George's is the oldest surviving one in England. Owned by the National Trust, it is home to a theatre and the **King's Lynn Festival**.

By contrast, **Trinity Guildhall** by Saturday Market, was completed in 1421, its unusual checkerboard façade of limestone and flint makes it one of the most-pictured buildings in East Anglia.

Both guilds stored their wine in the undercroft (cellars), and feasted in the main hall. Medieval guilds filled a strange role; part town council, benevolent society, bank, and trade union, with religious overtones. This was too much for Edward VI so in 1547 he disbanded them and seized most of their assets; after all, Henry VIII had robbed the monasteries and friaries a decade earlier, a move which prompted the name change from Bishop's Lynn to King's Lynn.

In 1571 the old Trinity undercroft, its timber ceiling replaced by brick barrel-vaulting, became a prison, surviving as such until 1937.

King John Cup. Trinity was restored in the 1950s, the cellars now the **museum** holding, among other items, the King John Cup, the oldest secular loving cup in England, made around 1340 in the reign of Edward III. The **King John Sword** has inscriptions mentioning John and Henry VIII, but is probably Tudor. **King John's Charter** of 1204 is definitely original, and the **Red Register**, recording 14th-cent wills and deeds, is one of the world's oldest paper books.

The museum's exhibits include the **Nuremberg Cup** of 1634 and a tankard given to Samuel Gurney Cresswell in 1853. The locals believe Samuel, born in Lynn, was the first man to sail the North-West Passage, but history credits Roald Amundsen in 1903–05.

The regalia rooms are open year round (not Sunday Nov-Apr) for a fee; access from the neighbouring **Town Hall**, built 1895. The **Tourist office** is the old Jail House, built in 1784 and in service as the police station until 1935; you may go in the cells.

Ouse reclaimed. In Norman times the Great Ouse swept in a vast curve a mile wide as it approached Lynn. Straightening began in the 14th cent but the present channel was completed in 1853. **Thoresby College** in Queen St has a slate marking the coastline in 1300; the college was founded by the merchant Thomas Thoresby for teaching 16 priests, and its Great Hall is on view by appointment: tel 01553.763871.

REBUILDING THE TOWN

The town was gradually rebuilt a second time between 1550 and 1650 in clay brick, fired in kilns in Gaywood and West Lynn. The Corporation bought the bricks at £5 per 1,000 in 1613 – yet in 1437 it had bought 200,000 bricks for the South Gate for £50. Thatch was forbidden, so roofing tiles were shipped from the Netherlands, no problem for a maritime town.

The **Hanseatic Warehouse** was built in the 1480s, in brick, by German merchants on land given by Edward IV. **Marriott's Barn**, also near the river, has stone walls to withstand floods, its timber superstructure probably being 16th-cent German work. The warehouse was renamed St Margaret's House after Edward Everard bought it in 1751 for St Margaret's Church. The Hanseatic League? It was a north-German medieval protection society for merchants which collapsed during the Thirty Years' War, 1618-48.

Customs House. One of the classic buildings of Lynn is the Customs House on Purfleet, financed by Charles Turner of Warham but built in 1683 by local man Henry Bell; look on the south wall for the sculpted heads wearing corn ears and grapes. This was one of many local buildings featured in the box-office flop *Revolution*, filmed in the town.

Ferry. North of Purfleet is Ferry Lane, which leads to the passenger ferry operating the half-hourly service to West Lynn for a small fee.

THE TOWN WALLS

Bishop's Lynn had been well-defended since its beginning: at the south by Friar's Fleet (known as the River Nar by outsiders, the Esk by townspeople, and the Puny River by people from Middleton); west, by the Great Ouse; north by Purfleet and Fisherfleet. That left only the landward approach from the east.

In 1294 Edward I gave Lynn the right to levy *murage*, a tax on inward goods to raise money for building the town wall, *mur* in French. The wall was an earth embankment, but the gates, and the parts protecting Turbe's town, were of stone. East Gate, demolished in 1800, stood on today's Littleport St, and Dowshill Gate was near Alexandra Dock.

South Gate. Two gates survive. **North Guanock Gate** to the east has been much restored, but **South Gate** is the most impressive medieval gateway in East Anglia (others are in Castle Acre and Norwich) as traffic still surges through it.

The present gate was built in 1437 of brick faced with stone, probably on the site of the first gate of Edward III's reign. Maintenance for that original work fell on villagers as far as Castle Acre and Stoke Ferry, but the people of Lynn were responsible for the later gate. Robert Hertanger, a London mason, was paid £100 in advance to build it, but drank the money instead and was sacked: the corporation had to hire another mason.

In the Middle Ages the gatekeeper charged tolls on goods entering town, closed the gate at dusk and, when bubonic plague was around, kept out all visitors who couldn't prove a need to enter. Robert Anthony, appointed in 1509, was also 'cleanser of the muckhills' as the town's rubbish was dumped outside South Gate.

Later gatekeepers took a percentage of the tolls, but on 25 March 1723 the last keeper was dismissed as tolls were abolished on that day. The council still appoints a gatekeeper, whose only task is to open the building to the public Wed, Jun-Sep, 1100-1500, free.

The Honest Lawyer. Lynn has a popular lawyer who claims to be honest: it's the name of a pub by South Gate.

Civil War. None of Lynn's defences was tested in battle, but South Gate was threatened during the Civil War of 1642–49 when Royalists under Sir Hamon L'Estrange seized the town and were besieged by Parliamentarians led by the Earl of Manchester. After Lynn's water supply was cut, it surrendered.

Red Mount Chapel. The Red Mount Chapel was never part of the defences though it's nearby. Built around 1485 by friars, it supplied lodging to pilgrims who had sailed into Lynn and were about to walk to Walsingham. After the dissolution of the friaries in 1538 and the collapse of the Walsingham Pilgrimage, Red Mount Chapel lost its customers, yet it has survived, an octagonal building on its own small mound.

WITCHCRAFT

Maggie Read's Heart. Margaret Read had been burned at the stake in Tuesday Market in 1590, her heart bursting from her body and flying across the square. Look for a diamond-shaped brick high in a wall on the north-east corner of the market, showing where Maggie's heart struck. Legend claims it then bounced down Water Lane and into the river.

Normally the crime of sorcery was punished by hanging, but if a witch had used her powers to kill anybody, then the penalty was death by fire.

Elizabeth Housegoe died that way in 1598, as did Mary Smith in 1616. Mary had allegedly bewitched Elizabeth Hancocke who died after Mary called "a pox to light on you." A prosecution witness was the Rev Mr Roberts who, in 1615, had laid a water main to the house that Maggie Read's heart struck.

And in 1646 Lynn Corporation paid £5 to Matthew Hopkins, the Witchfinder General, for finding two witches in the town and seeing them hang in Tuesday Market.

CAPTAIN VANCOUVER

Lynn's 11th-cent seagoing merchants shipped out wool, fish and salt, and returned with millstones, furs and timber. A century later, Brughes and Ghent had joined the trade which was concentrating on wool and cloth as East Anglia prospered. The abbeys of Ely and Peterborough sent out vast quantities of wool – in 1267 Lynn handled 1,406 sacks of it worth £3,440. The previous year Lynn imported wine from Gascony, including 50 tuns (12,600 gallons, 57,000 litres) for Henry III.

Lynn saw commerce as its main income and soon it was importing exotics such as Russian beeswax, Finnish timber, Icelandic fish – and pilgrims for Walsingham. By 1604 Lynn was almost as busy as Bristol, with 96 shiploads in and 159 out.

Smuggling was an inevitable sideline, a typical case being the discovery in 1718 of a load of brandy in a man's home. He was whipped around the town.

King's Lynn's South Gate was built for medieval traffic but now takes juggernauts and coaches.

The old Customs House on King's Lynn's Purfleet.

Greenland. A few years later Lynn was sending five whalers each May to Greenland, returning in July – the **Greenland Fishery** building in Bridge St was built in 1605 – while other trade took in Dorset lead, Norwegian furs, dyes from Picardy, and the shipping of corn to Scotland, cloth to Denmark and wool to Italy.

George Vancouver. It was the perfect background for George Vancouver, born in 1757 on New Conduit Street, son of the deputy Collector of Customs at Purfleet.

Vancouver had every incentive for a seagoing career. In 1771 he joined Captain Cook aboard *Resolution* for a four-year voyage around the world. In 1776 he signed on as midshipman on Cook's last voyage, aboard *Discovery*. They discovered Hawaii, naming the islands from John Montagu Sandwich, First Lord of the Admiralty, and Vancouver was among the sailors who retrieved Cook's body after the islanders murdered him. He was back again in 1791–92, persuading the Hawaiians to become part of the British Empire; he also took Western Australia whose natives could not object.

Vancouver, B.C. Then he sailed to Canada, negotiated that the Spanish cede to Britain territories from the Alaskan Panhandle to Great Salt Lake; some of it became British Colombia, whose largest city is now Vancouver – but the man from whom it is named died at Petersham, Surrey, aged 40.

LYNN'S CHURCHES

The oldest surviving church is **All Saints'** known to its Saxon founders as All Hallows. All Saints' Day is 1 November, a public holiday in most of Europe, but Britons celebrate the day before, All Hallows' Eve. The present All Saints' was rebuilt in the 14th cent, with little since. Its main interest is the **anchorhold**, a cell in which hermits volunteered to be locked for the remainder of their days. Records show that the anchorhold was occupied in 1272, 1477 and the 16th cent, the inmate's needs been satisfied by a servant living next door.

St. Margaret's. The mother church is St Margaret's, founded in 1101 by Herbert de Losinga, but little of the original remains. In the 12th cent two towers were added at the west end, to be heightened in the 14th cent. Soon the north-west tower began leaning as it was on poor soil; in 1453 the clergy built a larger tower around it, for support. Despite this warning, in the 16th cent the other tower had a 258ft (78.6m) spire added.

And then came the storm of 8 September 1741 which demolished steeple and tower, hurling the masonry onto the roof. George II and Sir Robert Walpole, MP for Lynn, each gave £1,000 and the Borough raised £3,500 by taxation. The tower was replaced, but not the steeple.

The nave has several treasures; the richly-decorated pulpit was probably made by Matthew Brettingham, the man who built the main staircase at Holkham Hall. He included the Hebrew letters of the Tetragrammaton, the name of the 'Unmentionable One,' Jehovah or Yahweh, often shown as YHWH. Look for the Mayor's official pew; also for the reredos (ornamental screen) showing Felix, a preacher who was befriended by badgers after being shipwrecked at Babingley. Felix became the first Bishop of Dunwich, and Felixstowe is named from him. The side chapel is said to have

Time and tide wait for no man, certainly not at St Margaret's Church, King's Lynn.

England's largest brass memorial, this to Adam de Walsoken who died in 1349.

Tides and floods. Lynn has always been subject to high-tide flooding, so the clock on the south tower shows the tides, the 12 letters spelling LYNNHIGHTIDE. It was installed in 1603 but recent floods have worsened. Tidemarks in ascending order read: March 1961, March 1949, March 1883, Jan 1953, Jan 1978. The sea may be rising, but the coast is certainly sinking.

St Nicholas's Chapel. St Nicholas's Chapel, the town's third church, was built in the 13th and 15th cents and is now used only for concerts in the King's Lynn Festival. The chapel suffers from severe subsidence and is seldom open.

LYNN MISCELLANY

Numbers **28, 30** and **32 King St** hide the remains of a medieval stone hall. At the Market Lane junction with Chapel St is **Lattice House**, once a block of shops and homes in a long building, and later one of the town's 400 inns, a reminder that until modern times the water supply was undrinkable.

Rotten borough. Lynn was among the 100 English boroughs granted the right in 1558 to have its own Member of Parliament – but Lynn had *two* members. At one time both seats were under the patronage of Thomas Howard, fourth Duke of Norfolk, and were available only to the landed gentry. In 1675 Robert Coke of Holkham spent £10,000 on his election, and later MPs included Lord George Bentinck, leader of the Protectionist Party, and Lord Stanley, son of the Earl of Derby. The Derby in question is a hamlet on the Isle of Man where a certain horse race was begun.

Caithness Glass. Not many tourist attractions are on industrial estates, but Caithness Glass is in business on the Hardwick Road Estate, offering tours of the glassblowing works. The firm has several factories in Scotland but moved here a few years ago. The works closed briefly, but are now open again.

BEYOND THE TOWN

WEST OF KING'S LYNN

Cross the Great Ouse into the Fens and take the A17 almost to the county boundary. At Terrington St Clement you will find **Wellbanks Orchid World** and 7,500sq ft of glasshouses full of orchids, open daily for a fee. **Ornamental Conifers and Heathers** is nearby, with an acre of nursery open daily except midwinter.

The village also holds the Rev Tony Clements's **African Violet Centre** described in full on page 16.

William d'Albini began Castle Rising, and Edward II's widow is supposed to haunt it.

EAST OF LYNN: CASTLE RISING

Castle Rising is both castle and village. Before 1066, 'Rysyng' was owned by Stigand, the Lord of the Manor of Snettisham, the man who crowned Harold in 1066. The modern village is small, rebuilt in the 12th cent to make way for the castle. The church, which has its tower at the transept crossing, has plaques to several members of the Howard family which produced numerous Dukes of Norfolk. One such was the son of Baron Templeton who married Mary Howard then changed his name to hers – after all, the Howards had lands in three other counties.

The nearby **Babingley River** was a tidal creek in medieval times, hence the ditty:

> *Rising was a sea-port town when Lynn was but a marsh.*
> *Now Lynn it is a sea-port town and Rising fares the worse.*

The rhyme gives you some idea of the Norfolk pronunciation for 'worse.'

Rotten borough II. Rising was another rotten borough, with two MPs from 1558 to 1832; our first Prime Minister, Sir Robert Peel of Houghton Hall, was one of them.

RISING CASTLE. Rising Castle was begun around 1138 by **William d'Albini** whose family came from Normandy; much of the earthwork was done a little later, proved by the discovery of the buried half of a silver penny minted between 1158 and '80: it was cut to make two halfpennies.

Bigod family. William d'Albini was also Lord of the Manors of Buckenham. Happisburgh and Snettisham, and married Maud Bigod, of the family which soon produced the Dukes of Norfolk. Albini built the priory at Wymondham where, in 1833, workmen found what is believed to be Maud's lead-lined coffin. William and Maud's marriage ended with her death in childbirth but their surviving son, William II d'Albini, married the widow of Henry I and so gained Arundel Castle in Sussex. A much later daughter of the Earl of Arundel married into the Howard Dukes of Norfolk, which resulted in the Norfolks moving the family seat to Arundel.

The Albini family continued to hold the earldom of Sussex, and the manors of Arundel, Buckenham and Rising, later adding the vast estates of the Clare family of Clare, Suffolk – who owned County Clare, Ireland. The fourth William d'Albini was with King John at the signing of Magna Carta, but he died on the way home from the Fifth Crusade in 1221.

By the mid-13th-cent the castle needed major repairs, which were probably done by Robert Montalt, Lord of Rising from 1299 to 1329. He sold the castle to Edward III for 10,000 marks (£6,666) in 1327, his widow selling her remaining rights to Queen Isabella in 1331.

Ghost. Edward II was murdered in September 1327, allegedly by a red-hot poker up his anus. His widow, also Isabella, was imprisoned in Castle Rising on suspicion of complicity. She went mad, and her screams are said to haunt the castle to this day.

Black Prince. Rising eventually passed to the Black Prince, the son of Edward III. He died in 1376, the year before he would have become king, but he had decreed that Rising be held in perpetuity by the Duchy of Cornwall. In fact it stayed duchy property only until 1544 when Henry VIII gave castle and manor to Thomas Howard, third Duke of Norfolk, and his son Henry, the Earl of Surrey.

King Henry beheaded Earl Henry in January 1547 and promised the duke he would die on 28 January. But early that day the king died, and the duke was spared. The tombs of Thomas, Henry, and the Arundel daughter, are all in Framlingham Church, Suffolk.

THE CASTLE TODAY. Castle Rising stayed in Howard ownership until 1958 when it passed to the State, and it's now maintained by English Heritage. Only the keep and the gatehouse survive, but the keep is large and in good condition, as befits its other name of 'donjon,' meaning 'power.' There are ruins of the Norman church of Rysyng, abandoned when the village was moved and rediscovered in the 19th cent. The massive earthworks which surround the building are intact, enclosing around 12 acres (5ha), but little remains of the curtain wall that stood on top.

The keep has similarities with that of Norwich Castle, and both may have been copies of the castle at Falaise, Normandy. The keep is 78.5ft long, plus 20ft for the forebuilding which guards the main door (total 30m) by 68.5ft (21m) wide, with walls rising 50ft (15m).

The steps to the main door at first_floor level are impressive, but the great hall, at the same level, lost its grandeur with its floor and roof, leaving a hole 47ft by 23ft (14m by 7m).

The pre-bypass road to Hunstanton ran through the village, with a nasty bend at **Onion Corner**, named from the smell drifting off the fields. Cross the Babingley River and you are in the Sandringham Estate.

THE SANDRINGHAM ESTATE

Albert-Edward, Prince of Wales, was house-hunting. His parents, Queen Victoria and Prince Albert, wanted him to have a country home when he was 21. On 4 February 1862, Prince Edward saw Sandringham Hall and asked his mother to buy it: the price was £220,000.

The prince extended the hall and in March 1863 brought his bride here, Princess Alexandra of Denmark. Further extensions were needed, then the prince demolished the main part and built anew.

In November 1891, fire destroyed 14 upper-storey rooms, but the prince proceeded with plans to hold his 50th birthday party here a few days later. The repairs inevitably gave him the opportunity to add more bedrooms.

The prince's son, later George V, brought his own bride to a small house in the grounds and later renamed it York Cottage. As their family grew, so the cottage was extended, and it was here that George VI was born. The building is now the estate office.

Christmas message. The Royal Family tends to use Sandringham House as a winter retreat, and it was from here that George V made his first Christmas Day radio broadcast in 1932, with Queen Elizabeth giving her first televised Christmas message from here in 1957.

There were further extensions between 1973 and '76, and in 1977 the Queen decided to open the house and grounds to the public.

THE ESTATE.

Sandringham Estate covers 20,600 acres (8,334ha, 32sq miles) and includes the villages of Anmer, Babingley, Flitcham, Gt Bircham, Shernborne, West Newton, and Wolferton, and part of Dersingham, with 600 acres open free to the public as a country park with marked walks. Sandringham is not a village, although it has a church; Domesday recorded it as *Sant Dersingham*.

The estate is the Monarch's personal property and is run commercially, its profits helping maintain the house. Much of the land is worked by tenant farmers, but the Queen farms 3,310 acres, has 1,954 acres under forestry, and 243 acres as stud farms. There's also the 117-acre fruit farm at Appleton, popular for pick-your-own.

SANDRINGHAM HOUSE

Sandringham House is an elegant country home built of carrstone and brick and splendidly set in gardens of 90 acres (36ha) with mature trees. Visitors can see some of the house interior including the main two-storey saloon with minstrel gallery, the lady-in-waiting's small drawing room, the main drawing room, the dining room and the ballroom. For a full description read the official guide available in the souvenir shop.

Outside, most visitors' first glimpse of the estate will be the elegant wrought-iron **Norwich Gates**, made for the Great Exhibition of 1862, later a wedding gift for the Prince and Princess of Wales.

Museum. The Coach Houses, fire station and estate power house, all to the east of the main house, have formed the Sandringham Museum since 1973. The Royal cars include a 1900 Tonneau, the first car bought by royalty; a 1913 saloon; a 1928 brougham; and a 1937 shooting-brake, all built by Daimler.

The museum also has the estate fire engine, a display of big game trophies, and horse racing memorabilia.

THE VILLAGES

The first village after Castle Rising is tiny **Babingley**, whose sign shows **St Felix** in his ship Legend claims that Felix built the first church in East Anglia here, around 630, to be followed much later by a stone church abandoned in 1861. The present church of corrugated iron and thatch was the gift of Edward VII.

The countryside here is very sandy, supporting conifers, heathers and rhododendrons, where grass snakes and deer can be found. It is a truly beautiful landscape, especially in May and June.

WOLFERTON. Two turnings left a loop road leads to Wolferton, noted for its railway station, church, and village sign, one of many in the county.

The wolf is the legendary **Fenrir**, an evil beast who terrorised the villagers. The Norse god Woden sent them a cord to restrain Fenrir – but he would wear it only if a man put his arm in the beast's mouth. Tyr volunteered and, when Fenrir realised he was shackled, he bit off Tyr's arm. Rough justice!

Station Museum. The railway runs no more, but the station is a museum of royal rail memorabilia. The royal retiring rooms built in 1898 are retained, and you can see Victoria's travelling bed and many other souvenirs of the days of glory. Open daily Apr-Sep; phone 01485.540674.

Wolferton Church. St Peter's Church, built in carrstone around 1310 near where Felix came ashore, has several oddities. There are 13th-cent stone coffins by the door, and a stone seat recalling the days before pews, when the old and infirm leaned against the wall. The south side of the chancel has a small window set low to allow lepers to follow the service from outside.

WEST NEWTON. Many of the estate staff live in this village, which has a large water tower built for Appleton Farm in 1877, with homes for two families beneath the tank. When Appleton Hall was burned out in 1707 the Paston family, famed for its 'Paston Letters', quit – and the church of St Mary was abandoned. Its round tower is more likely Norman than Saxon.

FLITCHAM. Flitcham was originally Felixtown, another reminder of Bishop Felix. Abbey Farm is on the site of an Augustinian Priory built around 1251.

Never stick your arm down a beast's throat or, like Tyr, you'll lose it.

ANMER. This tiny village has one of the steepest hills in Norfolk.

SHERNBORNE. Shernborne's church is on the site of East Anglia's second-oldest chapel – another relic of Felix's presence. The modern church was rebuilt by the Prince of Wales, later Edward VII. The village sign shows St Thomas de Shernborne, who became chamberlain to Henry VI's queen, Margaret of Anjou.

DERSINGHAM. The sea is now 2.5 miles away, but Dersingham was a fishing port in medieval times, and Henry VI granted its fishermen the freedom of the seas. On land, there were seven manors after the Norman Conquest, but the tide has turned, for the Royal Estate now owns much of Dersingham.

St Nicholas's first recorded vicar came in 1106; there's a 12th-cent coffin lid inside the door; and there's a wooden chest almost 7ft long which was made before 1360. Yet the church itself is pure 14th-cent, with a 15th-cent hammerbeam roof.

Great Barn. The churchyard holds the Great Barn, bearing the date 1671 July 31; the county council maintains it.

Modern attractions are **Dersingham Pottery** in Chapel Road where porcelain and stoneware are thrown by hand (open daily); and **High Farm** where Suffolk punch and similar heavy horses still work the land. Come for a demonstration, and a ride on a hay wagon, Easter-Sep Mon-Fri. Refreshments available.

BEYOND THE ROYAL ESTATE

Gt BIRCHAM. Gt Bircham has been home to humanity since the Bronze Age, proven by burial mounds on the common, which yielded bones and jewellery.

Bircham Mill. The village has the only working windmill in this part of Norfolk, although the county had 300 in 1800. Built in 1846 on a site occupied since 1769, the mill is open to the public daily Apr-Sep. Climb the 52ft tower with its five floors on a breezy day and see the machinery working – and admire the view. Visit the coal-fired bakery, built around 1800, and sample its bread. Or try the tea room and gift shop.

You may have pony rides from here, or hire a cycle by the hour or day. Phone 01485.23393.

War Graves. King George VI unveiled a cross in 1946 at the War Graves Cemetery by the church of St Mary the Virgin. Here lie 66 Allied air crew, 11 German, and one servicewoman. This church retains its box pews, and above a Norman arch are the Royal Arms of George III.

BIRCHAM NEWTON. The village is tiny and its much-restored 13th-cent church is among the smallest in the county. No porches; no windows on the north and just four on the south, while the east window is small. The floor is brick, and the Victorian box pews are still in place. In short, All Saints' would make a good setting for a film on Dickensian poverty.

Yet it was not poor. Nelson's daughter Horatia married Philip Ward, the rector of the Birchams, and brought up a large family at Church Farm.

R.A.F. Bircham Newton. The Royal Flying Corps had a base here in 1916; rebuilt in 1929 it was a major World War Two airfield. 617 Squadron was here to practise with Barnes Wallis's bouncing bomb for the Dam Busters raid, but the RAF moved out in 1960; seven years later the **Bircham Newton Training Centre** began teaching people how to build brick walls. Trouble is, somebody else has to knock them down again.

BIRCHAM TOFTS. Domesday recorded the village as *Stoftstan*, referring to its stony soil. The parish merged with Bircham Newton in 1719 but the church remained in use until 1941.

LEZIATE. East of Lynn along the B1145 is Leziate, a hamlet amid beautiful heatherstrewn countryside; even the sandpits are full of wildlife from martins to lizards. **Gayton** has little to offer as its windmill is derelict, but its name contrasts with that of **Grimston**, suggesting it may be the Devil's town.

Nearby **East Walton**'s church has some box pews but the priory ruins are on private land and so inaccessible.

The B1145 leads onto **Gt Massingham**, whose church has an enormous tower. St Andrew's in **Lt Massingham** was founded by the Saxons, but the oldest part is a solitary Norman window. Sir John L'Estrange was buried here in 1517 because of a clause in his will beginning *if I die within five miles of Massingham . . .*

HARPLEY. Harpley sits south of the A148, its Church of St Lawrence rebuilt by Sir Robert Knollys (Knowles), commander of the English troops in the wars with France under Edward III and Richard II. Its interior is bare and forbidding – and big – and the 15th-cent pews and 14th-cent rood are still in place.

Bishops. Earlier churchwardens had a liking for history, as the church's chronology of bishops of East Anglia shows:

Felix, 630-647	Thomas 647-653
Boniface 653-669	Bisus 669-673.

Then the diocese was split into two: **Dunwich** in the south, **Elmham** in the north:

North Elmham	**Dunwich**
Bedwinnus (673-9)	Etta (673-)
Northbert	Astwolf
Headulac (-731-)	Eadferth
Edelfrid	Cuthwin
Lanferth	Alberth
Athelwolf (-811-)	Eglaf
Unferth	Herdred
Sibba (-816-)	Alsin
Humferth	Tidferth (787-816)
St Humbert	Weremund
(killed by Danes 870 or 871)	Wibred

HOUGHTON HALL.

Harpley leads to Houghton Hall, closed in the mid-1990s for a major refurbishment in which several million poundsworth of treasures were sold. It was built in the 18th cent for Sir Robert Walpole, the first Prime Minister, but is currently the seat of the Marquess of Cholmondeley and when open to view, is a masterpiece revealed.

The Hall. The hall exterior is of strict Palladian design, based on the style of Andrea Palladio, but inside, the decor and furnishings outshine those of Sandringham House and rival the best in the country. Walpole devoted the ground floor to hunting while the first floor, reached by grand steps to the main door, was for taste and elegance.

The second floor had the bedrooms, including the State Apartment. There are few records of who slept here, but it is known that in 1732 Walpole spent £1,200 on gold lace for the Green Velvet State Bed.

The **White Drawing Room** is probably the most lavish part of the house, its detail beyond description in a few words – but see the gilded plasterwork and the furniture by William Kent, who furnished much of

NORFOLK SHIRE HORSE CENTRE

David and Jonquil Bakewell opened the Shire Horse Centre at West Runton in 1982 as a working museum and a showplace for draught horses, not as a commercial farm; the only crops grown are for the animals.

Daily at 1115 and 1500 Sun-Fri, Apr-Oct, one or more of the centre's horses is harnessed up and gives a half-hour demonstration of what life on the land was like until mechanisation came in the 1950s. In addition, a calendar of special events offers ploughing, drilling, harrowing, tedding (hay turning) and the corn harvest, in season, with shoeing, a foal parade, and sheep dogs at work at any time of year. Events are subject to the weather.

The Shire Horse developed in the English midland 'shires' and served as draught animal and war horse from medieval times until two generations ago. It is the largest and heaviest horse in the world, standing up to 19 hands (6ft 4in, 1.93m) and weighing more than a ton. The Shire Horse Centre has other heavy breeds, such as the Suffolk Punch, the Clydesdale and the Percheron, and representatives of several pony breeds: the Shetland, Highland, Fell, Dales, Welsh, Exmoor, New Forest and Dartmoor, plus the Connemara from Ireland.

Mini-ciné And there's a 40-seat video room showing a 30-minute film; the small animals enclosure for kids, ducks, geese, lambs, and pot-bellied pigs; the adventure playground; and the café and gift shop. Additionally, children can ride around the village in a horse-drawn cart, and there's the **West Runton Riding School**, open all year. 01263.837339. See also page 77.

SHEILA ROWSE DESIGNS

Converted traditional Norfolk barns make an attractive home for Sheila Rowse Designs, a business which produces and prints its own graphics on a wide variety of textiles. The products range from aprons to oven gloves, tea towels to bags, screen printed by hand on the premises. Visitors may watch the work in progress on weekdays during the tourist season.

All the designs have a rural theme, as seen in the picture opposite, from the *Roosters* range; another favourite is *Cats*. Originality is the hallmark, often with a subtle hint of humour.

Shop. Sheila Rowse sells her products into retail shops around the country and abroad, but they're all available in the large retail shop at **The Textile Centre** on the B1388 pilgrim route through the centre of Great Walsingham; the address is Hindringham Road, Gt Walsingham, NR22 6DR; 01328.820009. You can also browse around many other goods, including clothing, books, cards and unusual gifts. The integral café offers homemade baking and ploughman's lunches daily throughout the season. Car park; facilities for disabled. Open daily mid-Mar-mid-Nov. See also page 68.

The Norfolk Shire Horse Centre (above) re-creates the days of one-horse-power; © Jarrold Publishing. The `Rooster' range of Sheila Rowse's designs (below).

The MUCKLEBURGH COLLECTION

Midway between Sheringham and Blakeney, the Muckleburgh Collecton is the largest private military collection of its kind in the UK that is open to the public. It started with around 40 military vehicles on opening day in May 1988, but now has well over 1,500 exhibits of all kinds, from radio sets and uniforms to 14 working tanks.

Muckleburgh, with eight display halls – you can forget the weather – is one of the most-visited attractions in north Norfolk. In fact, the buildings were the former NAAFI (Navy, Army & Air Force Institute) canteen for the original Weybourne Military Camp.

The hardware comes from a wide range of countries and conflicts, including Belgium, Czech Republic, France, Ireland, Israel, Italy, Netherlands, Norway, Switzerand and, of course, the old USSR. Theatres of conflict range from World War Two to the Falklands campaign, the Gulf War of 1991 – and there are exhibits from the 18th century.

Weapons. Weapons and vehicles range from the Willys Amphibious Jeep, to anti-tank guns, ambulances, rocket launchers, together with to the smaller exhibits in the model room. The diorama room re-creates WW2 graphically, and glimpses a Fighter Command airfield as its aircrew scramble to intercept the enemy. A special hall remembers the **Suffolk and Norfolk Yeomanry** founded in 1794 by Viscount Townshend of Raynham.

Into battle. Tanks are demonstrated in action every Sunday, and daily during the summer season. During your visit you can relax in the licensed restaurant and listen to the music of the forties and fifties. Open daily Mar-Oct. 01263.588210.

Picture shows an anti-aircraft gun at maximum elevation. See also page 82.

●

Holkham Hall.

Royal Throne. The most outstanding treasure must be the Royal Throne which the Queen uses at the State Opening of Parliament. Beside it is Prince Philip's throne – an inch shorter. Shorter still are the thrones for the Prince and Princess of Wales.

The entrance hall is impressive in the extreme, 40ft (12m) in every dimension; and the parlour mantelpiece shows the genius of Grinling Gibbons.

Model soldiers. The Cholmondeley Collection of 20,000 model soldiers is claimed to be the best in the world. See the Battle of Culloden Moor in 1746, the Battle of Isandlwana in the Zulu War, and a campaign in the Western Desert in 1942 led by Lt Rocksavage – now Lord Cholmondeley. Outside are stables with heavy horses and Shetland ponies, peacocks on the lawn, and an *enormous* park.

Sir ROBERT WALPOLE. Robert was the fifth of 19 children, born on the Houghton estate in 1676. He went to a private school in Gt Massingham, then Eton and Cambridge; while he was there, sampling the alehouses, his two older brothers died, leaving him heir to the estate, At 24 he married the daughter of the Lord Mayor of London, and claimed his inheritance in 1710 on his father's death. He was 35.

Whig. He followed family tradition by entering Parliament: he *owned* the Castle Rising seat. He was, of course, a Whig. Moving on to the seat for King's Lynn, which he also owned, Walpole rose quickly through the ranks: Secretary at War, Treasurer of the Navy. But in 1712 he was in the Tower of London, convicted of bribery involving a mere £2,000; in later life he claimed that bribery and corruption were essential elements in the business of statesmanship, and every man has his price.

Queen Anne dies. In 1714 Anne was dying and the ruling Tories were negotiating the succession of James Edward, a Catholic. Walpole and other leading Whigs burst into the royal bedchamber and persuaded Anne to let them take over the administration. This bold strategy gave not only a new government but a new monarch, as the Whigs proclaimed George I. True, he spoke only German, but he was a protestant.

Prime Minister. Walpole became First Lord of the Treasury and Chancellor of the Exchequer in 1715, and so becoming prime among ministers. He was thus the nation's first Prime Minister, a post he held for 22 years, helped now and then by his brother-in-law Turnip Townshend.

Walpole saved the nation from bankruptcy after the South Sea Bubble, but found himself obliged to give the new king, George II, £100,000 a year from the Civil List. A grateful king gave Walpole his town house at 10 Downing St, but Walpole accepted it as the official residence of the First Lord of the Treasury, which it still is.

Walpole resigned in 1742, became the First Earl of Orford (Suffolk) with an annual pension of £4,000. He died on 18 March 1745, leaving the Houghton estate deep in debt.

3: HUNSTANTON

Roman Norfolk

HUNSTANTON IS A HAPPY RESORT. It sits on a sloping greensward, it has the only red-and-white cliffs in England, and it's unique for an east coast resort in that it faces *west*. At low tide you can see Lincolnshire and the 272ft (80m) tower of Boston's church – the 'stump'

The resort began in Victorian times and depended heavily on the railway. Edward, Prince of Wales, came here to recover from a severe attack of typhoid and so publicised the town. The good beach has a scattering of carrstone rocks giving it a wild look popular with children.

But the town has problems. There's little industry, so Hunston – as the locals call it – depends on tourism and retirement homes. You can see the town in half a day, but there's plenty to keep families busy all week. Hunston has more entertainment than any Norfolk resort except Gt Yarmouth, yet it's still a quiet country community. In fact, there are *two* Hunstons: the Old one is where the coast swings east.

Origins. Bishop Aelfric of Elmham gave land at 'Hunstanes tune' to St Edmund's Abbey at Bury. The abbot built **St Edmund's Chapel** in Old Hunston to mark the spot where the saint came ashore; today the ruins (open daily) are near the lighthouse, which is not open. The saint is also shown in a window of St Edmund's Church in the new town.

With the Normans in control, Ralph was lord of the manor, under Roger Bigod, the Earl of Norfolk. Ralph's daughter married Roland le Strange, and for the next 900 years the **L'Estrange** family has lived in Old Hunston, latterly at the Hall, a moated mansion damaged by fire in 1853. There are family tombs and brasses in St Mary's Church in the old town.

Beheaded. St Mary's records recall that in 1286 Nicholas Bragge was beheaded on the second conviction for theft, the only known instance of this punishment for larceny in England.

ENTERTAINMENTS. Hunston lost its pier in 1978 but it has added numerous attractions. Foremost is **Kingdom of the Sea** on the South Promenade, which also has a **seal hospital**. The Kingdom is a twin to the attraction at Yarmouth, both open daily except Christmas. Phone 01485.533576.

Its rival is the covered-in **Oasis** offering a wide range of sports from aquaslide to tennis. 01485.534227.

Go take a cruise to **Seal Island**, a sandbank in The Wash, aboard a

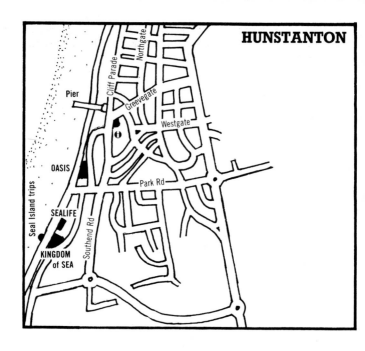

HUNSTANTON

Pier

Cliff Parade

Northgate

Greevegate

Westgate

OASIS

Seal Island trips

SEALIFE

Southend Rd

Park Rd

KINGDOM of SEA

Traction engine rallies are popular now these giants have retired from the daily scene.

catamaran – or even on a DUKW (pronounced 'duck'), a wartime amphibian troop-carrier. You might even have the chance to fly in a Cessna from the beach to Skegness. More details are at the **tourist office** in the town centre: 01485.532610.

HEACHAM

You're in for a big surprise at Heacham. Your clues begin in St Mary the Virgin's Church where you can see a monument to Princess **Pocahontas**.

Now, the Rolfe family was to Heacham whan the L'Estranges were to Hunston. John Rolfe, born 1585, sailed to Virginia in 1609, losing his wie and baby in a shipwreck. He went alone to Jamestown, the first English colony in America, founded two years earlier. And there he fell in love with 14-year-old Pocahontas.

Go further back. Captain John Smith (who had worked at Lynn) helped build Jamestown. He had gone exploring, was captured by native Americans and taken to their chief, Powhatan, who ordered Smith to be killed. Powhatan's daughter, Pocahontas, threw herself at Smith and so saved his life. She became the link between the natives and the Europeans, and was the first native to be baptised.

Bring back Rolfe. He and Pocahontas married, and grew tobacco in Jamestown. Their son Thomas was born in 1615 and the next year the family sailed for England. They certainly came to Heacham, and legend claims they planted a mulberry at Heacham Hall. And they went to London where Pocahontas was presented to James I.

In 1617 they were in Gravesend preparing to sail back to Virginia, when Pocahontas died. She was buried in the town's St George's Church, while Rolfe boarded ship. He was to die in 1622 in the Massacre of Henrico.

The Pocahontas memorial was put in the church in 1933; Heacham Hall was burned down in 1941; and the last Rolfe died in 1990.

The church. Let's go back to the church. Note that the tower is in the central crossing? How was its weight supported? Now see the enormous buttress that has done the job since 1802. The single bell, cast in the 12th cent, is probably the oldest in East Anglia, and the brass chandeliers, given by the Rolfes, are a copy of those in St Mark's, Venice.

Trades Union. On Guy Fawkes' Day 1795, 110 poor farmers and 106 day labourers met in Heacham church to organise their labour and so claim a reasonable wage – 39 years before the Tolpuddle Martys. The Heacham attempt failed because the Anti-sedition Law was introduced that same month. Is it coincidence that Moss Evans, the former leader of the TGWU, moved to Heacham in 1987 and was elected district councillor in 1991?

NORFOLK LAVENDER

Roughly opposite the church is Caley Mill, home of England's only commercial lavender farm (there's another on Jersey). Founded in 1932,

The growing coastline: sand dunes and marram grass on the western coast of Norfolk . . .

the company now has around 100acres (40ha) on which it grows several types for distillation of the oil, producing half a ton in a good year. French lavender farms around Grasse squeeze 1,000 tons a year.

Bath. The Romans perfumed their bath water with lavender, and the plant's name comes from the Latin *lavare*, 'to wash.' The Tudors used lavender with charcoal as a toothpaste, and with beeswax as a polish. Later it perfumed tobacco and soap. Norfolk Lavender sends its oils to Yardleys, the perfumiers.

The lavender grounds are open year round, free, with guided tours Apr-Sep; the gift shop and tea rooms are open daily, except Christmas; and the conservatory shop for buying plants, Easter-Sep. There are coach trips to more distant fields Jun-Aug. Phone 01485.70384 for more details.

BEACH. Heacham has vast beaches to north and south, of sandcastle quality inshore, verging to mud at low water level. Caravan sites dominate the coastline inland of the creek, which was once Heacham Harbour; today there's no access to the sea. Car park.

SNETTISHAM

Snettisham is the village that has the quarry that yields the carrstone that's used around the district. But it has three tourist attractions as well.

PARK FARM. This is a genuine working farm on the eastern edge of the village where on 329 acres you can see the lambing in March and April, the deer calving in June and July, and all other farming activities in season. And a ride through the deer park; and venison and eggs for sale. Plus a children's play area, craft shop, and tea shop. Open from lambing to harvest.

WATER MILL. The long road down to the shore passes the water mill, *erected in a time of scarcity by public subscription for the benefit of the neighbourhood, 1800,* according to a sign on the front. Now restored, the mill again grinds wheat at restricted times, and sells the flour. Show the children the Lego exhibition and the ducks on the millpond.

SNETTISHAM COASTAL PARK. At the end of the road is the Coastal Park, an important wildlife refuge run by the district council. 1.8 miles (3km) long and covering 143 acres (58ha), it removes human pressure from a fragile environment. The warden is usually on duty daily Apr-Sep, but the park is always open, with lavatories near the entrance and a hide midway along the 'blue trail.' The warden lives at Village Farm, Ingoldisthorpe (01485.41239).

A sample from the many birds you may see here, in season: curlew, brent goose, heron, merganser, short-eared owl, sanderling, snipe, turnstone and widgeon.

With habitat ranging from reed to open water, you may also see these butterflies and moths: burnet, large hawk, meadow brown, orange tip, and small copper. The flora is mainly salt-tolerant, including sea holly, sea lavender and glasswort – better known in this area as the edible **samphire.**

Beach. The beach is ideal for sandcastles at high water mark, but low

. . . and groins to check erosion of cliffs near Sheringham on the eastern coast.

water exposes two miles of sand gradually changing to mud. There is no beach south of the village as the Great Ouse mudflats come this far. *Beware going out too far and being caught by the incoming tide – it comes in faster than you can walk.*

Rose and Crown. Back in the village, the Rose and Crown is a charming 14th-cent coaching inn.

Snettisham treasure. The village's fourth attraction is in the British Museum; it's a gold bracelet of c70BC which was found here. Man has probably lived on this spot since Neolithic times.

INGOLDISTHORPE. The charming village of 'Inglesthorpe' has nothing to delay you – even the church is redundant.

THE NORTH COAST

HOLME next the SEA. East from Old Hunstanton the first village is Holme, a pleasant place off the main road. It has a wide beach ideal for sandcastles, with pools at low water. Access on foot across the golf course, and there are no servcies to spoil the natural beauty. Pack your gear in; pack your rubbish out.

Church. The 15th-cent church of St Mary has a tower 76ft (23m) tall, almost separated from the nave which has an austere interior. Built by Henry Notingham – one 't' – who was a judge to Henry IV, it was always too big for the village. In 1778 much of the nave was demolished, resulting in today's bizarre plan. Notingham's brass is the main feature of interest:

> Henry Notingham & hys wyffe lyne here
> yat maden this chirche stepull & quere [choir]
> two vestments & belles they made also
> christ hem save therefore ffro wo
> and to bring her saules to blis of heaven
> sayth pater & ave with mylde steven.

There is no longer a 'stepull' and the Notinghams' graves are outside, as the church vanished from over them.

Napoleon. Ann Jane le Clerc of this parish had a daughter who married into the family of Lord Nelson. But Ann was a niece of General le Clerc, uncle by marriage to Napoleon Bonaparte, Nelson's enemy.

Peddars Way. The village is the northern end of Peddars Way, the Roman road from Colchester to Lincoln via a ferry across The Wash. The road is traceable to Knettishall, near Thetford, and from there on is pure speculation.

Bird observatory. The village has an observatory run by the Norfolk Ornithologists' Association, with the Norfolk Wildlife Trust reserve nearby: see chapter 1.

THORNHAM

Boadica, queen of the Iceni, destroyed Colchester in 62. The Roman governor Paullinus retaliated, killing 80,000 Britons, after which Boadicea took her own life. The Romans colonised East Anglia, building forts – including one at Thornham. Its ruins were discovered in 1948 by a study of aerial photos, but a few artefacts have also been found. Excavations soon revealed a Saxon cemetery with 22 skeletons, all of which went to the Castle Museum, Norwich.

Church. The Saxons began All Saints' Church – their porch and priest room above it, remain – but most of the present work came after the Black Death of 1348–'50. Thornham's mass grave for plague victims is by Staithe Lane, leading to the harbour.

Neglect hit the church: by 1845 the roof had collapsed and the bell was in the churchyard, but by 1900 the restoration was complete. A large colony of bats moved in after World War Two, so the vicar and congregation reduced them by attacking with tennis rackets – thankfully, attitudes have changed.

A windmill and separate water mill were on Staithe Lane in the 13th cent. Both have gone, but a model of the windmill is in the church.

Henry VIII's dissolution of the monasteries in 1536 saw the seizure of Thornham Manor, which he gave to his physician, William Butts, co-founder of the **Royal College of Surgeons**.

Ironworks. The Hogge family, who built Thornham Hall in 1788, ended with a daughter who married into the Ames Lyde family. She did the unthinkable for 1887 by starting an iron foundry in the village. Surprisingly, it succeeded, but never paid its way for years. Then in 1899 25 men were producing, among other things, small gates for Sandringham House and decorations for Balmoral Castle. The next year it was gates for the Royal Pavilion at the Paris Exhibition, and soon orders came from around the Empire.

In 1914 Mrs Ames Lyde died and the Great War started, each a fatal event to the business. The smithy closed in 1920 and is now the local service station.

Lifeboat Inn. The 16th-cent Lifeboat Inn was a working farmhouse for generations, and qualified to become an alehouse as it had a window opening onto the road – a strange ruling. Its name marks the coming of the Hunstanton lifeboat. As smuggling was rife, the village had Customs men in lodgings, some inevitably staying at the inn.

Beach. The beach is difficult to reach along a mile of the Norfolk Coastal Path. It's therefore empty but excellent.

TITCHWELL. Titchwell has its RSPB reserve (see chapter 1) and an excellent beach. The church has a round tower, but stone from Normandy for the windows. Is it a Norman tower in Saxon style, or a Saxon tower with Norman additions? Nobody knows.

BRANCASTER and SCOLT HEAD ISLAND

Little is visible of the Roman fort at Branodunum, built to suppress the Iceni, and it was not until 1960 that the Romano-British cemetery was discovered nearby.

This beautiful village, whose name may mean 'burned castle', knows nothing of its Roman origins and lives by tourism and shell-fishing. The 14th-cent church of St Mary the Virgin is a successor to the one that Edgar the Peaceful (959–975) gave to Ramsey Abbey, and has a 7ft (2.1m) telescopic font cover. Elsewhere a plaque recalls the village's lifeboats *Joseph and Mary,* (1874–'93, saved 3), *Alfred S Gerith* (1893–1914, saved 6) and the final one, *Winlaton*, which never saved anybody.

BRANCASTER STAITHE. This hamlet, now bigger than Brancaster itself, developed as Scolt Head Island grew, and flourished in the 18th and 19th cents. In 1797 it had a malt house, claimed to be England's largest, but it was demolished in 1878. Sailing ships moved grain, coal and malt, but today the harbour is devoted to pleasure boats.

Mussels are still farmed in the harbour, brought here for three years from The Wash, and whelks are dredged from the sea bed 15 miles away.

Beach. A good road leads to the beach (pay car park), where the sand is perfect – and you could find remains of a forest that was drowned when the sea rose at the end of the Ice Ages.

National Trust. The National Trust, which owns almost everything between the coastal path and low water, from Brancaster to Burnham Harbour, including most of Scolt Head, has an **information centre** at the staithe, open Mar-Aug (times vary). Cycle hire is available on daily or weekly rates, and contact the warden (01485.210719) for renting self-catering accommodation.

SCOLT HEAD ISLAND. This remarkable island is around 3.7 miles (6km) long, and has been growing throughout recorded history. Its northern coast is a series of sand dunes protecting the salt marsh; it is uninhabited and little-visited, necessary as the ecology is so fragile.

The National Trust bought Scolt Head from Lord Leicester of Holkham Hall in 1923, with the Norfolk Naturalist Trust buying the eastern tip in 1945: the Nature Conservancy Council leased the entire island for 99 years in 1953.

Here is England's largest breeding colony of Sandwich terns; there are other tern species, gulls, plovers, oystercatchers, and others. A marked trail assures minimum disturbance, with the ternery closed in May and June.

Access by boat is from Brancaster Staithe, depending on tides and weather. Dogs not allowed Apr-Aug.

Samphire. The salt marshes from Lynn to Brancaster grow large areas of samphire, an edible seaweed on sale in fishmongers' in high summer. Samphire, pronounced *sam-fuh*, is a corruption of the French *Saint Pierre*, and is known to botanists as glasswort. Some of the samphire beds are now protected, so ask before you harvest.

Remove the roots and rinse well, then boil or steam the samphire until the flesh is tender. The easy if inelegant way to eat it is by pulling the flesh off with your teeth, but you may try a fork instead. Eat it within a day as it cannot be preserved.

INLAND FROM HUNSTANTON

DOCKING. The largest inland village for miles was once called Dry Docking as it is on a hilltop almost 300ft (90m) above sea level, with no permanent stream nearer than Fring. The villagers dug a well in 1760, and at 237ft (72.2m) they struck water, which was then sold at a farthing (0.6p) a bucket. A pump came in 1928, but proved erratic, so in 1934 people bought water from Bircham Newton airfield at a ha'penny a bucket.

Church. The oldest part of St Mary the Virgin's is the chancel, built before the Black Death, but an earlier church may have had links with Aelfric, Bishop of Elmham in 1038. As a Norman order owned Docking Rectory in 1415 Henry, fresh from the Battle of Agincourt and distrusting the French, seized it for the crown where it stayed until Henry VI gave it to Eton College.

STANHOE. Stanhoe is a tiny village, but its 14th-cent church of All Saints has a wall tablet remembering Sir William Hoste of Burnham Market who fought in the Battle of Lissa (Croatia, 1866). It doesn't explain why he was there.

The shingle bank that runs out to Blakeney Point.

Other villages. Poor **Fring**'s only claim to fame is that it was mentioned in Domesday – but so was **Sedgeford**, where the Saxon church's round tower has survived, entombed in the later square tower. **Ringstead** has one of those rare Norman round towers on St Peter's Church; it's now the only part that survives, in the grounds of the former rectory. That was Ringstead Magna; Ringstead Parva and its church of St Andrew have completely disappeared. Strange – the present church is also dedicated to St Andrew.

Views. The road from Ringstead to Holme offers splendid views across The Wash, and on a clear day you can see the Lincolnshire Wolds.

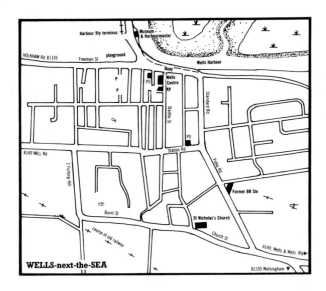

4: WELLS-NEXT-THE-SEA

Nelson's Norfolk

WELLS MADE MUCH of its living in medieval times by plundering shipwrecks. As the definition of a wreck was a vessel on which nobody had survived, those men first at the scene often had some unpleasant business to do. Wells men acquired the nickname *bite-fingers* for their time-saving method of removing rings from corpses.

Although it is 'next-the-sea,' *with* the hyphens, Wells has lived on maritime trade until recent times, with the earliest mention in the 13th cent. The north Norfolk ports, including Blakeney and Cley, could manage vessels up to 160 tons, which was larger than any of Columbus's ships: the *Santa Maria* displaced only 90 tons.

Harbour Commissioners. An Act of Parliament in 1675 created the Wells Harbour Commissioners, who could then charge 6d (2.5p) for every tun or last landed. A tun was 252 gallons if wine, less if beer, and a last was 640 gallons of grain. An Act of 1835 changed the duty to a shilling (5p) a *ton*, not 'tun,' of the ship's registered tonnage.

Lifeboat. An Act of 1844 allowed the commissioners to buy property and build the present quay, which meant the demolition of 28 cottages and sheds. The same Act decreed that a lifeboat be provided, with a £2 a day fine if it were not seaworthy: this rule continued until the RNLI brought its own boat in 1869.

Sea wall. Back in 1758 one Sir John Turner began draining the marshes by Warham, but in 1858–59 the Admiralty gave Lord Leicester of Holkham Hall permission to build a sea wall north from town, cutting off 588 acres (2.37sq km) of marsh, as well as tidal access to Holkham village. Holkham harbour died and Wells began silting – because the sea wall was dead straight, and nature does not allow straight lines.

Silting never became a major problem and so Wells continued trading, becoming prosperous from 1850 to 1914, although the railway took some business from 1857. Cargos were mainly coal, malt and barley, with Guinness long a buyer of the malt. Trade changed after 1918 with potash in and sugar beet out.

Whelks. Hitler's war stopped almost all activity as Wells became an Air-Sea Rescue base. Whelk fishing recovered quickly after the war, with Wells supplying 60% of the nation's needs, but general trade was in the doldrums with around 14 ships a year. Favor Parker bought the quayside in the 1970s and increased the import of animal fodder, but exports were still slack.

Examples? In 1985, 248 shiploads in, totalling nearly 100,000 tons – but 9 shiploads out, at 4,150 tons. In 1968, 218 shiploads in and the last one to go out; 1989, 121 in; 1990 51 in; 1993 and 94, 18 in. The *Albatross* is the only vessel now calling.

The problems are twofold: there is a draft limit of 10ft (3m), attainable only on spring tides – and dredging is uneconomic. It's the chicken-and-egg business again.

Pleasure craft. But private boating is on the increase, with many permanent moorings in the outflow creek. Boats capable of more than 15 knots (28kph) are allowed in harbour only for shore access, and all craft must obey the 5mph speed limit. Jet skiing is banned in the harbour, and windsurfers must have a licence. At the outflow's end, skiers and windsurfers are allowed – but in designated areas. **The channel current is fast**, so weak swimmers must be careful.

As Wells has the only commercial harbour between Lynn and Yarmouth, it is popular with private yachtsmen on passage; phone 01328.711744.

Disasters. Tuesday, 27 February 1898. The naval gunboat *Alarm* heaves to and launches its shoreboat. Shoreboat overturns in rough seas, six men drowned. Coastguard boat goes to the rescue, capsizes – five more drowned. Eleven men therefore died in an exercise to deliver a copper lamp to the harbourmaster!

Favor Parker's silo on the quay has flood markers for 11 January 1978 (16ft 1in, 4.91m above high tide) and 31 January 1953 (16ft 10in, 5.13m), when a ship was lifted onto the quay; the dates are also recorded at St Margaret's, Lynn.

Museum. Wells Museum, which opened in 1991 behind the Harbourmaster's office (Sat, Sun, Wed) has photos of the stranded ship among many maritime exhibits. Nearby is a box on a pillar, set at the waterside. It's the National Rivers Authority's **tide measure** which relays information by phone in Morse code.

Wildfowling. Wells was probably the best place for wildfowling in the early 20th cent, and it was popular with the aristocracy who took up to 15,000 pink-footed geese in a season.

Harbour Railway. The town has two 10.25in-gauge (26cm) railways, both owned by the same man. The Harbour Railway runs along the sea wall, from the museum to the coastguard lookout and lifeboat station by the beach – there's also a good pay car park here. Trains operate Apr-Sep with up to 18 return trips per day, serving Pinewood Caravan Park.

Beach. The beach is one of the best in England, and is an official Area of Outstanding Natural Beauty – pine woods, and sand dunes pegged by marram grass planted by the Coke family of Holkham Hall. There are no services at all, but that's as it should be.

WELLS and WALSINGHAM LIGHT RAILWAY

The other 10.25in railway ran its first service in March 1982 along the route of the Wells & Fakenham Railway which closed in 1964.

British Rail took up the track and sold the land, so the WWLR had to start almost at the beginning, even to moving 3,000 tons of rubbish from a cutting and spreading the remainder, leaving a 1-in-29 gradient, among the steepest in Britain. The line started with one locomotive, *Pilgrim*, an 0-6-0 side tank engine with two cylinders working to 125psi (8 bar), custom-built by David King of North Walsham. It had to haul four coaches with 42 passengers up that 1-in-29 grade.

Trouble was, the WWLR was too successful. A fifth carriage was added in 1985, giving a payload of 52 but taking *Pilgrim* to its limits. Soon *Weasel*, an 0-6-0 powered by a Ford petrol engine was added, followed by another steam loco, the *Norfolk Hero*, two 2-6-0's mounted back-to-back. Its four cylinders take 140psi and it's 20ft 4in (6.21m) long by 34in (0.864m) wide.

Timetable. The WWLR covers its four miles (6.4km) of track in 25 minutes. Season, Easter-Sep, daily, up to six return journeys per day.

The old station in Wells is now **Burnham Pottery**, while the old signal box is the new station. If that's confusing, the old station in Walsingham is now a church!

And Finally . . .

St Nicholas's Church. Wells's patron saint is Nicholas, who cares for children, fishermen, pawnbrokers, merchants, travellers, and a few others, and who was the original Santa Claus, a name which is corrupted from the Dutch *Sint Niklaas*. Old Nick gave three bags of gold to pay for a merchant's daughters' marriages – hence the pawnbroker's symbol. He's supposed to have tossed the money down the chimney – hence dear Santa.

The first church on this site was probably built around 1229, the first known vicar came in 1302, and the place was rebuilt around 1460. Then in 1879 lightning struck the tower and the church was burned out. St Nicholas's was rebuilt by 1883 to the same design, at a cost of £7,000.

Two objects that escaped the fire are a brass eagle-style lectern and the church chest. The lectern had vanished years before – hiding from Cromwell's men, perhaps – and was found buried in a field: a pickaxe made a hole in it. The chest of 1635 was dragged clear but still has scorch marks.

The parish register records the baptism of John Fryer, sailing master of H.M.S. *Bounty*, made notorious by Captain Bligh. Fryer's headstone was removed and his grave is now lost.

Playland. Wells is for the lover of solitude, wide beaches, nature, country walks, sailing and cycling. Playland, near the quay, is the only

The Wells and Walsingham Light Railway claims the world's smallest-gauge public-service track: 10.25 inches.

concession to amusements, and it's just for the youngsters.

Tourist Office. Staithe Street, near the quay. Apr-Oct, hours vary. Phone 01328.710885.

HOLKHAM HALL

Let's begin with Robert Coke. Born in Mileham, near Fakenham, he was a lawyer at Lincoln's Inn. His son Edward, born 1550, studied at Norwich and Cambridge. Called to the bar, he later married Bridget Paston and built **Godwick Hall**. He also led the trials of Raleigh and Guy Fawkes, but that's another story.

Soon the family produced Thomas Coke who did the Grand Tour then, in 1718, decided to build the ultimate mansion on the family estates. Eleven years passed before work began – and that was just the obelisk.

Now let's move to the Earldom of Leicester, a title held by Simon de Montfort among others. Several families qualified for the earldom and it eventually passed to Thomas Coke who, by then, had planted the avenue of beeches. Soon the hall itself was to be built and, in time, the estate would grow to 3,200 acres (5sq miles exact, 12.95sq km) and be part-surrounded by a brick wall 9 miles (14.5km) long.

Thomas died in 1759, the hall passing in 1766 to **Thomas William Coke**, born 1754, but the title passing to the Townshend family. Thomas William became Member of Parliament the year he inherited Holkham, and stayed there with few breaks until 1833. In 1837 he became Earl of Leicester and in June 1842 he died; he's buried in **Tittleshall**.

Houghton Hall was the home of Britain's first Prime Minister, Sir Robert Walpole. Blickling Hall (below) has associations with Anne Boleyn, but she never lived in this stately home.

Hunstanton's red and white cliffs face west. Sandringham House is a beautiful country home set amid splendid gardens.

Coke of Norfolk. Thomas William, better known as Coke of Norfolk, revolutionised British farming by introducing a four-year-rotation – wheat; turnips; barley with clover undersown; clover. It introduced a forage crop and a root crop, so livestock could be kept overwinter instead of being slaughtered in autumn and salted. The extra dung increased fertility, and turnips appeared on cottage tables.

Turnip Townshend. Yet he couldn't have done it alone. Charles Townshend of Raynham Hall had studied turnip and clover cultivation in the Netherlands and so given Coke his raw materials. Charles was brother-in-law of **Robert Walpole**, but he is better known as Turnip Townshend. His grandson, also Charles, when Chancellor of the Exchequer, imposed taxes on the New England colonists and so prompted the Boston Tea Party, but that's also another story.

Jethro Tull. Both men owed part of their success to Jethro Tull, who invented the horse-drawn seed drill. And all three relied on the collapse of the feudal strip system, in favour of a man owning a set piece of land outright and not holding it by grace and favour from the lord of the manor. Parliament had already passed the Enclosures Act which brought major changes to the countryside: hedges separated the smaller fields, and cottages went up on the new holdings. Half the farmland had been enclosed by 1750, and statistics show the results. In 1700 England produced 13,000,000 quarters of wheat, but in 1820 the yield was 25,000,000. A quarter? That was 64 gallons.

Building the Hall. But what of Holkham Hall? Building began in 1734 and was to take 27 years, William Kent designing both Holkham and Houghton. Kent saw this hall as a giant H, the vertical strokes each 344ft (105m) long and outstripping Sandringham at its largest: after all, Coke of Norfolk entertained up to 700 guests at a time at the annual Holkham Shearings. They were the forerunners of the agricultural shows, but that's yet another story.

HOLKHAM TODAY. See the story on page 17.

Holkham Church. The village of Holkham clusters around the entrance to the long drive, but St Withburga's Church is inside the encircling wall. It stands on a mound built by the Saxons, hinting that a Saxon chapel was here. The plaques indicate the church is very much a memorial to the Coke family.

THE BURNHAMS and LORD NELSON

There are at least six villages in the Burnham group: Burnham Market, the main village above the tiny River Burn; Burnham Overy Staithe, where yachts can moor; Burnham Overy Town, which is no larger than a hamlet; Burnham Deepdale, no bigger; Burnham Norton, the 'north town' of the group; and Burnham Thorpe, birthplace of Admiral Horatio Nelson. Old

Ordnance Survey maps mark Burnham Westgate, Burnham Sutton and Burnham Ulph.

NELSON. Edmund Nelson was curate at Beccles in 1744 when he met Catherine Suckling, great-niece of Sir Robert Walpole. After their marriage they moved to Downham Market and thence to **Burnham Thorpe** in 1755. The sixth of their eleven children was Horatio, born 29 September 1758 in a house called the Shooting Box; he was seven weeks premature and was baptised within hours as nobody thought he would live.

The young Horatio studied in Norwich then moved to the Paston Grammar School in North Walsham as its owner was a friend of Horatio's mother who had recently died. A year into Paston School he heard that his uncle had been appointed captain of H.M.S. *Raisonnable*; Nelson begged his father to let him join the Navy as 'captain's servant.'

Nelson's early career took him to the West and East Indies, the Arctic and the Mediterranean, seldom coming back to Norfolk. He was commander of the *Boreas* when he met Fanny Nisbet on Nevis in the West Indies; they married in 1787.

Lady Hamilton. Nelson came home soon after, opted for half-pay and spent five years at Burnham Thorpe, sometimes visiting Houghton and Holkham halls. At last he was listed as captain of the *Agamemnon* in 1793, bound for the Med, where he met Lady Hamilton at the Court of Naples; the two were to become lovers.

Eye and arm. Nelson lost his right eye in 1794 off Corsica and his right arm in 1797 off Teneriffe, but he was now a national hero, a Knight of the Order of the Bath and Rear Admiral of the Blue – at the age of 38. He came home to Burnham Thorpe where Fanny nursed him for seven months, then he went off to the Battle of the Nile and earned the title of Baron Nelson of the Nile and Burnham Thorpe. His final battle was off Cape Trafalgar on 21 October 1805 where he was killed. His body was shipped home, but not for burial at Burnham Thorpe: he was destined for the crypt at St Paul's.

The Government gave Nelson's two surviving sisters £1,000 each; his elder brother received an earldom, £6,000 a year, and £100,000 to buy an estate: Lady Nelson received a pension of £2,000 a year – and Lady Hamilton got nothing: she died destitute in 1815. The nation got Nelson's Column in Trafalgar Square.

The *Lord Nelson*. The only pub in Burnham Thorpe is the *Lord Nelson*, which was in advanced decay when Les Winter took it over in 1966. He restored it to 1793 standards and made it into a Nelson museum. Winter's conclusion is that Nelson's private life was in such a mess – Lady Hamilton had borne him an illegitimate son – that he dressed in his finery and begged to be killed at Trafalgar. His final words to one of his captains before the battle had been: "God bless you, Blackwood. I shall never see you again."

A part of the Bygones Collection at Holkham Hall. Thursford and Muckleburgh have bygones of a different style.

THE CHURCH. All Saints' Church has a checkerboard finish on the east wall. A similar design is on the heraldic shield of Sir William Calthorpe in the chancel floor, inferring Sir William financed the east wall. The Calthorpes also left their mark on the churches at Anmer, East Barsham and Cockthorpe.

The crest of H.M.S. *Nelson* of WW2 is on an interior wall; her flag is in the north aisle with that of H.M.S. *Indomitable* of WW1. An ensign of the Nelson era flies from the tower on suitable days; the rood was a gift from Canada in Nelson's honour, while the cross and lectern were made from wood from H.M.S. *Victory*. The great chest was made from the Rev Edmund Nelson's pulpit; and the hassocks show *Victory* under full sail. Finally, a bust of Lord Nelson is on the chancel wall.

THE OTHER BURNHAMS

BURNHAM DEEPDALE. St Mary's Church has a Saxon round tower of c1040; the single bell was cast in Lynn in the 14th cent. The Norman font was damaged during restoration in 1791 and spent 40 years in the garden of Fincham Rectory. Now restored, its 12 panels show the farming year from the labourer's point of view.

BURNHAM NORTON. St Margaret's Church also has a round tower – so is it Saxon? There are deep architectural debates, but the concensus is that the tower dates from c1090. The nave and chancel are Early English and Perpendicular, taking them into the 15th cent, and the impression is that the interior would make a wonderful setting for a medieval film, except for the modern pews.

This church has other marvels: a bread oven in the north porch; the Jacobean pulpit has been claimed to be the best in England; and for most of its life the church had two rectors jointly appointed, making it a 'mediety;' and it's a mile from the village because the people abandoned the old village during the Black Death.

Burnham Norton Friary. Sir William Calthorpe helped found the Carmelite Friary in 1241; its name comes from Mount Carmel, near Haifa. The white-robed friars thrived, extended their home in 1249 and 1353, and at the dissolution in 1538 it owned 68 acres (27.5ha) — but the four remaining friars were broke. Lady Anne Calthorpe wanted to buy the place but Thomas Cromwell, Earl of Essex, first stripped out the lead, silverware, and the bells. The ruins passed to the Pepys family, relatives of Samuel, then to the Walpoles and finally the Cokes. Today it is an insignificant ruin by the school.

BURNHAM SUTTON-cum-ULPH. Two rectors for one church? Here we have two churches for one rector, and one parish. The name is easy. Ulf was a Dane who owned the manor, and Sutton is opposite to Norton.

BURNHAM WESTGATE. The church of St Mary the Virgin has a tower built c1310, and there's a window in memory of Sir William Boulton, a frequent benefactor to Nelson.

BURNHAM OVERY. Here's another example of a mobile village. The community began around St Clement's Church in **Burnham Overy Town** but as the Burn silted, seagoing vessels had to moor progressively further downstream. Eventually most people were at **Burnham Overy Staithe** (*staithe* means 'quay'). St Clement's was an oddity: its tower was at the crossing, but as it was too heavy for the walls the arches were bricked in, giving the feeling of two naves sharing a tower.

Mills. There are *three* mills in Burnham Overy; a private watermill on the B1155, and the National Trust mill on the A149 where the 18th-cent buildings include a malting floor.The last is a windmill (see map) built in 1816 and restored in 1986 for £26,000. None is open to the public.

The Hoste Arms. Sir William Hoste, born in the Burnhams in 1780, served under Nelson in several campaigns. The Hoste Arms is a 17th-cent hotel-restaurant in Burnham Market; the oldest hotel in the area, it was built to serve people coming to the local assizes. It also served as a staging post on the coaching run between Lynn and Norwich.

The CREAKES

Strange that two groups of villages should be named from alternative words for 'river,' particularly when they cluster around the same stream. The B1355 passes close to the ruins of **Creake Abbey**, an Augustinian community founded by Sir Robert de Narford and his wife in 1206. In 1504 all the priests died of the plague in one week, and the abbey ceased to function. It's now owned by English Heritage and is permanently open, free.

NORTH CREAKE. The church of St Mary the Virgin is probably 12th-cent, and the dedication is to the *birth* of Mary, while St Mary's in South Creake concentrates on her *assumption*. The nave is large and high, with an impressive hammerbeam roof, and traces of the rood stair remaining. Several surviving wills mention work on the tower; Nicholas Aleyn left £20 in 1435, Margaret Jeye left 26/8d (£1.33) in 1450, and Margaret Forster adding 10/– (50p) for the bells in 1470 – yet none of the bells predates 1744.

Yet another Sir William Calthorpe is shown in a large brass of c1505, holding a model of the church which he rebuilt.

Midshipman Easy. The Rev Thomas Keppell, rector from 1844 to '63, served under Capt Frederick Marryatt who wrote novels, notably the classic *Masterman Ready* (1841) in which Keppel was the model for Mr Midshipman Easy.

Forge Museum. The old village forge in Church Street has survived as a living museum of the blacksmith's art. In this rambling flint smithy the old-style coke forge is still heated by bellows, and old-time tools still hang on the walls. The tea rooms offer blacksmiths' lunches, and the River Burn runs through the tea gardens. Open weekdays in summer; 01328.738910.

SOUTH CREAKE. At the south end of the village, **Country Crafts and Gallery** mounts a permanent exhibition of paintings by local artists, and sells local craftware. Open daily; 01328.823563.

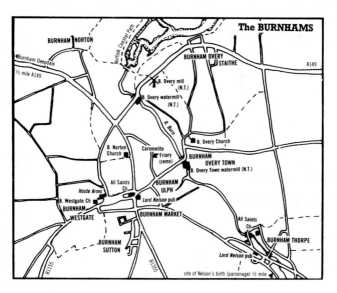

Sir Edward Coke's impressive memorial in Tittleshall Church. He built Godwick Hall; his family built Holkham Hall.

EAST FROM WELLS

WARHAM. The Burnhams have prepared us for more churches than there are villages, but the village of Warham went to the extreme and had *three* churches, all at the same time. **St Mary Magdalene** is the main one, amid the lime trees – you can easily miss the gateway. **All Saints** is a towerless church to the east, and **St Mary the Virgin** was to the west, but only the foundations remain. In addition, records mention a chapel. The answer is simple: there were originally three villages.

St Mary Magdalene has traces of Norman work in an arch, but building continued until the 15th cent. If you appreciate medieval architecture, look at the priest's door to the chancel, set in an inverted Y buttress. The interior is strikingly simple, with the box pews still in place.

The lists of priests is almost complete from 1278. Every one until 1377 has a name with the French *de*, 'of,' in it. This shows the Norman domination from 1066, fading gradually as the English language emerged from the mix of Norman and Saxon. By the way, the list includes Thomas Robert Keppel; here he was in charge of the combined parish of St Mary Magdalene and St Mary the Virgin from 1837. All Saints was a separate village until long after WW2.

The chapel is a testimony to the **Turner** family whom we met in King's Lynn. Charles Turner became brother-in-law to Prime Minister Walpole and his brother John was one of Lynn's two MPs, 'keeping the seat warm' for Walpole while he was in the Tower of London. If you don't believe this, read the inscription on John's tomb here.

Nepotism. There were times when **both** Lynn seats were held by Turners. The family bought the Warham estate in 1709, but in 1604 it was owned by Thomas Howard, the Earl of Surrey who was beheaded that year; Howard's tomb in Framlingham Church is claimed to be the most heavily-gilded in *Europe*. The last of the Turners died in 1780 and five years later the celebrated Coke of Norfolk bought the estate and demolished the hall. His last words are claimed to be about his two regrets in life: the demolition, and allowing hay-making on a Sunday.

Warham Camp. Go south from All Saints,' climb the hill, and look for a tiny "footpath" sign at the crest. A cart-track leads west to the vast double-ring earthwork of Warham Camp, covering several acres and with mounds 30ft (10m) high. Iron Age relics were found here in 1959, plus a Saxon midden. It's on private land, but you can visit it at any time.

STIFFKEY. Everybody knows that Stiffkey is pronounced 'Stewky.' Well, it isn't. The locals call it how it's spelled, and that's good enough. Stewky was the 16th-cent spelling.

Stiff or Stew, it's a charming little village once dominated by Stiffkey Hall, which the Bacon family began in 1578. At its prime around 1650 the hall had 80 rooms, but most of it was destroyed by fire in the 18th-cent; remains include the west wing and a gatehouse dated 1604.

Two churches. The village had a church in 1066 – but which one? St Mary's, as now is, was built c1310 and a second church, St John the Baptist's, was added in the 15th cent – each with its own rector. St Mary's was demolished in 1558 – you can see a trace of it in the churchyard – and St John's was extended. But which church stood on the original site?

COCKTHORPE. South of Stiffkey is the tiny village of Cockthorpe, whose church of St Andrew and All Saints is redundant, but a sign says where you can borrow the key. The church was built of rubble, and plastered, showing lack of funds. The inside is equally plain and simple, and there's another tomb to a member of the Calthorpe family – Sir James, who died in 1615. His wife, born Barbara Bacon, is remembered in a wall plaque which explains:

> *By her he had 8 sons and 6 daughters, in whose several marriages and issues the ancient glory of the name and family…did reflourish and is dilated into many of the best houses in the county.*

When Barbara died at the incredible age of 96 she had 193 descendants.

Two English admirals were baptised in this poor church: Sir John Narborough, who served under Blakeney man Sir Christopher Myngs in the Battles of North Foreland in July 1666. The other was Sir Cloudisley Shovell, who sailed under both Myngs and Narborough. He helped in the capture of Gibraltar in 1704 but his ship, the *Association*, was wrecked in the Scillies in 1707. In 1737 a dying woman confessed that Shovell was washed ashore alive, but she killed him for the emerald ring on his finger.

Cloudisley Shovell was reputedly born at Cockthorpe Hall, a 16th-cent house in brick and flint that held the Cockthorpe Hall Toy Museum, now closed.

LANGHAM. On the far side of the wartime Cockthorpe airfield is Langham, a small village that was known as Langham Episcopi after Pope Alexander III gave it to the Bishop of Elmham in 1176. Most of the present church is 15th-cent on 14th-cent foundations; it was originally dedicated to St Mary in 1603 but after a bishop of Norwich wrote that it was *whollie ruynatd and p'faned long since*, restoration began and St Andrew was added to the patron saints. Two of the three bells were cast at Blakeney in 1699 and 1702 – a strange place to find a bell-foundry.

The novelist **Captain Marryatt** lived in the village 1843–48, and was lost at sea on 20 December 1848.

LANGHAM GLASS: See the entry on page 81.

MORSTON. The people of the coastal village of Morston believed in the Second Coming. When the tower of the 13th-cent Church of **All Saints** was shattered by lightning in 1743, the villagers saw no need to repair it, for wasn't Christ due back quite soon? Only when they realised that Christ wasn't keeping the appointment, did they do the work.

Inside, look for the carving on the first corbel on the left, which shows the village gossip with his – or her – tongue out. The church is noticeably poorer than the Blakeney, Wiveton and Cley trio, where there was much better access to the sea in the Middle Ages.

Morston Quay. A lane leads to Morston Quay where you have a choice of boat to take you out to the seals on the sandbanks; there's also the chance to visit **Blakeney Point**, depending on season, tide, and weather. Go to the full extent of the path by the public toilets, or look around the village for ticket agents.

BLAKENEY and BLAKENEY POINT

The Domesday record of 1086 refers to **Esnuterle** and *Snuterlea*, meaning 'on a bleak location.' From this came the Middle English verb *sniteren*, 'to snow.' But where is, or was, Snitterlea village? There has been no coastal erosion here since the retreat of the glaciers, yet there's no trace of a community on an exposed headland.

The name *Blakeneye*, probably meaning 'black island, 'appeared in 1230, and in the 14th and 15th cents the village was known as Blakeney and Snitterlea. *Every* placename in East Anglia which ends in *-ey* or *-ea* (but not *-lea*), shows its Norse origins, as this word meant 'island.'

Finally, Snitterlea became the manor, church or friary, and Blakeney was the harbour. My theory was the village was built on the high land to the south, and the 'black island' could have been the growing Blakeney Point. But some people think the name came from Blekinge in south Sweden. Why not?

Busy port. The fact remains that Snitterlea-Blakeney was a busy medieval port, sending grain, and salt from the pans at **Salthouse**, in return for fish. Henry III granted Snitterlea a market in 1223, and in 1326 Blakeney was one of the country's 59 ports permitted to trade in horses, money and precious metals, which was an honour.

Edward III controlled the sale of fish at Snitterlea in 1358 as there was a big market at Blakeney; after this, the Blakeney name took preference.

St Nicholas. The size of St Nicholas's church infers that the community prospered. In Blakeney's case the nave probably served the village while the chancel served a **Carmelite Friary** established in 1296 and completed in 1321. The friary was north of the windmill – which is not a tourist attraction – on the site now occupied by Friary Farm.

Little is known of this friary, but St Nicholas's chancel a brass plaque bearing a Latin inscription, which reads in English:

𝕳ere lie the bodies of 𝕵ohn 𝕮althorp, knight, one of the founders (a mistake: it should read 'benefactors') of the convent of friars, and of 𝕬lice his wife, who died the 16th day of 𝕬ugust 𝕬𝕯 1508, on whose souls may

Sir John's will of 1503 states that his *Synnfull body* was *to be beryed in*

The Austin friars built the priory at Weybourne, but they moved out before Henry VIII arrived.

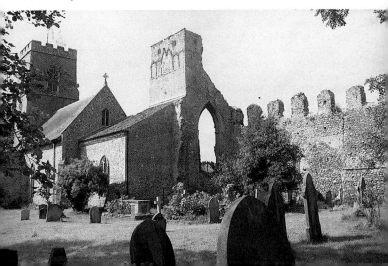

the White ffryes of Sniterlie, that is to say in the myddys of the chancell. And that's where he is.

The best-known associate of the friary was Sir John de Baconsthorpe, born 1290, educated at the friary and later practising medicine in Paris. But, of course, you've never heard of him.

Two towers. The nave was rebuilt c1435, making it distinctive from the earlier chancel. At the same time the great west tower was added, 104ft (31.7m) tall – but some sources claim 120ft (36.5m). One bell survives, cast in 1699. But the strange thing about St Nicholas's is its *eastern* tower, probably built along with the friary. Was it a lighthouse, as it's visible 20 miles out? But the other tower is taller. Was it a belltower? But the other tower is stronger.

Mappa Mundi. Records of 1368 show that the church had a Mappa Mundi, maybe like the one in Hereford Cathedral, but as it's gone, there's no way of answering that query either.

Parish records were in fair detail from 1538, but interesting margial notes come from 1727–'81, when Henry Calthorpe was rector. He noted the 'Great Snow' of five hours on 3 May 1698, the storm of 28 October 1772 when hailstones in Blakeney were '4in in girth,' and the 7ft (2m) sturgeon caught in Blakeney Pit, the channel north of Morston.

Census. The 1580 census gave Blakeney's population at 360, with the village owning 12 ships of tonnage ranging from 16 to 100; Wiveton had 13 ships, the smallest 40 tons; and Cley, with 450 people, had nine ships for fishing off Iceland.

Spanish Armada. The Privy Council, through the Mayor of Lynn, requested the three villages to provide a vessel or supplies to be sent against the approaching Spanish Armada in 1588. One story claims the trio refused the request, not so much from defiance of a royal request but suspecting extortion from Lynn. Another version claims all the men were away fishing off Iceland, while a third grants that Blakeney and Cley agreed to contribute.

We can be sure that the seamen of the three villages enjoyed a reputation in high places; the fishermen were exempt from the Press Gangs which snatched men off the streets for indefinite military service.

By the early 16th cent Dutchman van Hasedunck has been commissioned to reclaim the marshes at **Salthouse**, prompting Sir Henry Calthorpe to build a causeway from Blakeney to Cley, thus cutting Wiveton from access to the sea. After local protest the Privy Council ordered the bank to be destroyed – but it was too late to save Wiveton. Then in the 17th cent the bank was rebuilt, from Salthouse to Blakeney Point, so enclosing the harbour for evermore. The resulting silting of the Glaven gradually killed the commercial traffic, although Blakeney managed to ship coal and grain until 1914.

Guildhall. Blakeney's so-called Guildhall is a 14th-cent building close to the harbour; look for the little clock tower. The main feature is the undercroft (cellar) where you have an early example of a brick-built vaulted ceiling. This is all that remains – but it's hardly likely to have been a Guildhall. English Heritage owns it, and it's always open, no fee.

The quayside Blakeney Hotel, opened in 1923, replaced the Crown and Anchor pub, which the locals called the Barking Dickey. The Manor Hotel began life simply as the manor house.

Lifeboat. The Nofolk Association for Saving the Lives of Shipwrecked Mariners introduced an oar-driven lifeboat around 1820, based on Blakeney Point for a speedy response, though there could be delays in getting to the point; in 1860 eight men drowned in the harbour when answering a call. The RNLI took it over in 1861 but closed the station in 1925.

BLAKENEY POINT

The founders of the **Norfolk Wildlife Trust** bought 407 acres (164ha) of Cley Marshes in 1926. This, with the National Trust sector, puts the entire coastline and point under protection. Access to the point is by boat from Morston or on foot from Cley along the bank.

The peninsula is forever changing its shape, and is slowly expanding westward. At least 256 species of bird have been seen on the point, including terns, plovers, avocets, bittern and Lapland bunting. The point is also a vital feeding-ground for spring and autumn migrants. The colony of seals was reduced from around 700 to 200 by the epidemic of 1988, but numbers are increasing.

Blickling Hall is so big it's nice to take a rest.

Wiveton Church – but where's Wiveton?

Blakeney Point claims an impressive list of flora as well, with more than 190 flowering species recorded.

The old lifeboat house has survived and is now a refreshment hut Apr-Sep, while nearby is a toilet for disabled visitors who can travel along a 400ft (120m) boardwalk – *but the warden must be forewarned of a disabled visitor* on 01263.740480. Dogs must be on a lead at all times and are not allowed near the ternery Apr-Aug.

Sailing School. The Blakeney Point Sailing School which opened in 1991 offers instruction on small boats from the Mirror upwards, with most tuition being confined to the harbour. Phone 01263.741172.

WIVETON

The stone bridge near Wiveton church has long marked the head of navigation of the Glaven River, for it was built 1292 and is still in use. Its builder, William Storm, put a wooden bridge in Cley in the same year, but it has not endured.

Wiveton is overshadowed by its neighbours and no visitor would suspect its past glories, but listen to the story of *Susan, a good shippe of burthen . . . pressed into Queen Elizabeth's service in 1589 for service into Portugal, of which Thomas Coe of Claye went as Quartermaster.* Coe claimed the village had 19 other 'good shipps,' six having been built in Wiveton.

The church has several recently-discovered masons' marks showing sailing ships, and parish records name actual vessels: the *Gyles, Gift of*

God, *Trinity*, *Confidence*, and the *Mary James*. They ranged from fishing boats and merchant ships to men-of-war.

Harbour dues. An old document states that the *Lord of Wiveton Dulcis hath a bushel of coals, salt, or any measurable thing, of every ship that doth unload within the precinct of that manor*. In addition, English ships paid 4d to anchor, and foreigners 8d (19p).

St Mary the Virgin. The parish church, built at the head of the harbour late in the 13th cent, now overlooks the village green. A John Hakon wrote in his will of 1437 that he left 200 marks (£132) for þe makyng of a newe chyrche in Wyveton.' The letter þ is the old way of writing soft *th*, as in 'the,' and gave rise to the mistake of putting 'y,' making 'ye,' which was another form of 'you.' The character survives in modern Icelandic, and we'll meet it again.

But back to Hakon's bequest. It was enormous for the times: in 1482 a shipowner left 8d (3.5p) as contribution 'for the bells' and his widow left 6d for their repair. The same man, Robert Paston, left money to repair the chapel on the stone bridge; evidence of it survives at the bridge's south-west corner.

Orphan boy. Legend tells of a baby boy found on the green in the 16th cent, who was brought up by the entire village to share the costs. He was given the name Raulf Greneway and, says the legend, he became a rich merchant and founder of the Greneway Charity which left money for the local poor.

The charity survives, but the legend was wrong. Greneway was the son of a local farmer and merchant, and his brass in the church has the Greneway arms, the Grocers' Company arms, and his merchant's mark. His treasure chest and the Greneway charity date from 1558, the year of his death and the start of the parish records.

CLEY NEXT THE SEA

The church of St Margaret of Antioch is at the southern tip of Cley, surprisingly close to Wiveton Church, with Blakeney Church nearby; you can also see Glandford Church to the south.

St Mary's is impressively large for a tiny village, the nave and side chapels being 65ft by 115ft (20m by 35m), plus 28ft (7.5m) to the altar rail. The tower is short because it belonged to the earlier church on this site.

Sir John de Vaux had been granted 'Cly' Manor in 1265 as he already held Boston in Lincolnshire, then England's second-largest port – he presumably travelled between the ports by boat. Maritime trade was growing steadily, and after his death in 1288 his daughters rebuilt the church. John Ramsey, master mason of Norwich, was in charge of the work and in 18 years of intermittent work he produced the masterpiece still evident; the five-leaf-clover windows are based on those in the Palace of Westminster.

When Lady Petronella de Nerford (Narford?), de Vaux's elder daughter, died in 1326, Ramsey retired and the proposed new tower was abandoned, although his nephew continued with lesser work until the Black Death killed him in 1348.

South porch. The south porch, added after the Black Death, is a masterpiece of masonry. Look for the 16 armorial crests and, in the roof, an old woman throwing her distaff at a fox that has stolen a chicken.

Moving village. Cley is another village that moved. A major fire in September 1612 destroyed 117 houses around 'Claie' church. As the Glaven was already silting, the new homes were a little to the north, with further growth taking the village ever northward.

Bonnie Prince James. Cley seamen captured a Scottish ship in March 1406, taking Prince James of Scotland to France. As England and Scotland were temporarily at peace, the 11-year-old prince was sent on to London where Henry IV held him hostage. Kidnapping and piracy have never been far removed from the affairs of Norfolk seamen. The *Norfolk Chronicle* reported in December 1824:

> Thursday and Friday last, were seized on the beach and afloat, by the officers of His Majesty's Customs at this port (Cley), 120 half-ankers of geneva, 19 bags of tobacco, 10 bags of snuff, 10 boxes of segars, and two Chinese ornaments.

The same paper reported in 1883 a gunfight at Weybourne between smugglers and customs officers who seized 127 half-ankers of brandy and 3,500lb of tobacco.

MODERN CLEY. Cley today is a beautiful village troubled only by a narrow street and a tight corner. Along here is **Made in Cley**, a group of potters who make their wares on the premises; phone 01263.740134.

Cley Mill. Cley Mill, the artists' delight, was begun in 1713, and the best-known miller was the last, Steven Barnabus Burroughs, who worked it from 1840 to 1919 – 79 years. In 1921 it became a holiday home, renovated in 1983; it was caught in the 1953 floods, losing much furniture in the ebb tide. It is now open to visitors daily Easter-Sep, afternoons; for B&B Mar-Jan. The original stables are now self-catering apartments. 01263.740209.

Post Office. Have a look at the Post Office whose front wall appears to be built of animal bones.

Beach. The beach is mainly shingle, and there's a pay car park.

A mile east is a Norfolk Naturalists' Trust observatory for watching migratory birds; it's also the visitor centre for Cley Marshes, open Tues-Sun Apr-Oct. Car park.

GLANDFORD

Don't miss Glandford; it has one of the most beautiful fords in Norfolk. At the end of WW2 the county had hundreds of fords, most of which have succumbed to bridges. Glandford survived. The ford over the Glaven is around 100ft (30m) wide and too deep for cars; the bridge is for pedestrians.

All but one farmhouse and a few cottages was rebuilt early in the 20th cent by Sir Alfred Joddrell of Bayfield Hall to the south. He even rebuilt the church.

Baby church. St Martin's was in ruins in 1730. In 1875 the chancel was restored and in 1882 the cemetery reopened. Then along came sir Alfred who demolished all but the chancel and rebuilt to his own design, between 1899 and 1906.

This is no ordinary church. From inside it looks like an oversized doll's house, yet it has everything a parish church should have: hammerbeam roof, rood screen, carved pulpit, corbels in the ceiling – all carved from local oak and cedar. The carvers were Walter Thompson and Frank McGinnty, who carved each other at opposite ends of the frieze above the pew behind the door.

There is a carillon of 12 bells which rings out with the Westminster chimes every hour, and plays hymns four times daily.

Shell Museum. The Shell Museum is beside the churchyard. Sir Alfred built this in 1915 and gave some of the vast array of exhibits from around the world, some of which are now on the danger list. Open Mon-Sat, irregular hours, the museum is well worth a visit. Have you seen a nautilus elsewhere in Norfolk?

Signatures of some Norfolk worthies: Nelson Brontë; Sir Thomas Gresham; and Sir Edward Coke, builder of Godwick.

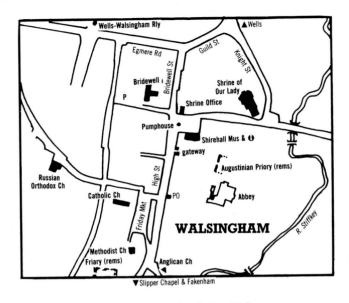

What should be on the Blakeney sign but a ship?

The Annunciation Altar in the Holy House at Little Walsingham and (below) the impressive church in the tiny weaving village of Worstead.

Norfolk Lavender near Hunstanton has Britain's only commercial lavender farm. The Benedictine Order moved into Binham Priory around 1091.

5: WALSINGHAM and FAKENHAM

Holy Norfolk

WALSINGHAM IS ENGLAND'S NATIONAL SHRINE. In medieval times it was the most important pilgrimage site in northern Europe, and a rival to Santiago de Compostela and even Rome. It died completely with the Reformation but its revival began in 1829, and Walsingham is now back on the pilgrimage and tourist trail. Tens of thousands come each year, but it cannot rival Knock, Lourdes, Fâtima or Santiago. If you're looking for it on the map, try *Little* Walsingham. Great Walsingham is a mile away and somewhat smaller.

Richeldis de Faverches. Lady Richeldis de Faverches, pious owner of the manor of Walsingham, had a vision of the Virgin Mary. In a dream she was taken to Nazareth of a thousand years earlier and shown the House of the Annunciation, where Mary heard of the baby she was to bear. Lady Richeldis had the vision twice more, convincing her she was to build a replica of Christ's home here in Walsingham.

She ordered a small timber-built chapel to be built between two wells, but unseen forces prevented the work. Lady Richeldis spent the night in prayer and in the morning the chapel was built – on another site.

Pilgrimage. While the Fransiscans built their priory at the south end of the village, Elizabeth, Countess of Clare, founded the Augustinian Priory of St Mary in 1347 on the site of Lady Richeldis's original chapel. Both orders served the pilgrims who came to Walsingham, as it was much safer and cheaper than going to the real Nazareth. Soon, indeed, Walsingham became known as 'England's Nazareth,' drawing pilgrims from hundreds of miles away.

Look at the Ordnance Survey map and trace the tracks those pilgrims made from King's Lynn and Heacham, from Burnham Thorpe, Wells and Blakeney. Many miles of these paths are today's tarred roads.

Henry III made a pilgrimage to the **Priory of Bromholm** at Bacton in 1233 as, ten years earlier, the priory, an extension of **Castle Acre**, had claimed to have a fragment of the True Cross. The publicity was good, as the Miller's Wife in the *Canterbury Tales* calls: 'Helpe, Holy Cross of Bromholme!' Other abbeys made the same claim, but Walsingham counter-claimed to have a sample of mother's milk from the Virgin Mary! So great was this absurd claim that for ages the Milky Way in the night sky was known as the Walsingham Way! Oh, yes – in 1241 Henry III came to Walsingham, the first of ten visits.

In the balance. Walsingham influenced politics when Edward I and the Count of Flanders signed a treaty of alliance here in 1296. Much later, Catherine of Aragon's sons had not survived infancy so Henry VIII made a barefoot pilgrimage to Walsingham to pray for his last ailing infant son.

The baby died. Henry decided it was Catherine's fault and so began his campaign for divorce, which led to the break with Rome and the dissolution of the monasteries, initially affecting all orders with an income greater than £200 a year. Walsingham was valued at £391.

Dissolution. The priory was wrecked. Sub-prior Nicholas Mileham and layman George Guisborough were executed. And the Walsingham Madonna was taken to Chelsea and burned. By 1538 it was all over: Walsingham was in ruins. Only the great arch of the priory's east window remained. Walsingham languished for generations. Then in 1829 came the Catholic emancipation, and in 1833 a group of Oxford intellectuals planned the Second Reformation: it became known as the **Oxford Movement**.

Soon, a few pilgrims were returning to Walsingham, even though almost everything was in ruins. But Charlotte Pearson Boyd bought the derelict 14th-cent **Slipper Chapel** in Houghton St Giles (2km south), and restoration was complete by 1934. Originally the final stopping-place for pilgrims from the south, it is now the **Catholic National Shrine** holding the **Holy Ghost Chapel**, open daily.

Pilgrims were coming in numbers by 1897, slowly building up to 10,000 in one procession in 1934. The pilgrimages ceased during WW2 but on 17 May 1945, six days after the German surrender, the US Army Air Force in Norfolk organised the first Mass at Walsingham since the Reformation.

Shrine of Our Lady. The rate of restoration accelerated. A duplicate of Lady Richeldis's shrine was built in Buxted, Sussex, in 1887, inspiring the local lad Alfred Hope Patten to devote his life to restoring Walsingham. He became a priest, was offered Walsingham in 1921, and stayed until his death in 1958. He achieved his ambition by rebuilding Lady Richeldis's shrine here in 1931, discovering the well in the process. The chapel, now the **Holy House**, holds the grand Annunciation Altar, based on the original priory seal held in the British Museum. This is the focal point of religious life in Walsingham and the start and finish of all pilgrimages.

Steps beside the Holy House lead down to the Holy Well where pilgrims are once again baptised, and many claim to have spiritual healing – see the plaques of appreciation. In 1938 the Holy House and well were incorporated in the **Pilgrimage Church**, which has 15 side chapels.

Prayers. Mass is held daily at 0730 in the shrine, 1130 in the chapel, and Shrine Prayers are offered at 1800. There are many other prayers, plus services at the Slipper Chapel, the Methodist and Catholic churches, the parish church of St Mary and All Saints, and the Russian Orthodox Church in the former railway station. There are summertime candlelit processions at 2015 on Saturdays, but the most spectacular are at the annual **National Pilgrimage** each Spring Bank Holiday, when thousands of people attend.

SECULAR WALSINGHAM

Little Walsingham was a small farming village until the revival of England's Nazareth, and it has adapted to its new role while retaining all its charm and character; the only modern housing is tucked away. A tour of the village on foot could start at the **Shrine Church**, from where we go north along Knight St, passing the **Refectory** of the College of Clergy, a half-timbered 16th-cent house. Left into Guild St for **Guild House** at the next junction. A right fork leads to Egmere Rd and the terminus of the W&WLR; there's no station.

Left takes you south into Bridewell St and the open area of **Common Place**. On your right is an alley leading to the former **prison**, built in 1787 on the site of a leper hospital. A 'bridewell' is a prison, taking its name from the jail which stood near St Bride's Well in London. This one had four treadmills and it's open, irregular dates.

Opposite the alley is a 15th-cent building, now a shop, beside which is the **Shrine Office** which arranges pilgrimages and accommodation; 01328.820255. The 16th-cent **pump house** is closed but can still draw water. At the bottom of Common Place is the 15th-cent **Bull Inn**, while on the south side, behind the limited parking space, is the **Shirehall Museum** and **Tourist Office**. The museum, 01328.820510, holds a court-house of the time of George III with a prisoner's cell, and other exhibits

The pump house in Common Place, Little Walsingham, was built in the 16th century.

on the story of Walsingham, and is high on the list of places you should visit. Open Easter-Sep, daily (hours vary), it is under the same administration as Cromer Museum. The tourist office (same times and phone) is the agency for guided tours of the village on Wed and Thur; for other times contact Scilla Landale, Westgate Farm, 01328.820250.

A walk down High Street is a visit to a living museum of architecture from the 15th to the 18th cents, plus the Georgian front of number 33 and the 13th-cent gateway leading to the few remains of the priory, open Apr-Sep, limited days.

An alley, right, leads to the **Market Place** and the 15th-cent **Black Lion** hotel. The south end of Market Place rejoins High St by the **Methodist Chapel**, built in 1794, then you are confronted with a Y-fork. Left, Church St leads to the parish church, damaged by fire in July 1961 and now restored. Right, the main road leads to the **Slipper Chapel**, with a side road to the ruins of the **Fransiscan Friary**, another of Henry VIII's victims.

GREAT WALSINGHAM

Overshadowed by its neighbour, Great Walsingham's Church of St Peter is worth a visit, but the main interest is probably Sheila Rowse's **Textile Centre**; for picture and details see page 32.

BINHAM

Binham had a priory that outshone the Augustinian one in Little Walsingham, and even in decay its ruins are impressive, the nave still serving as the Parish Church of St Mary.

Pierre de Valoines, nephew of Wiliam the Conqueror, founded the priory in 1091 as a dependency of the Benedictine Abbey of St Albans; Henry I endowed it c1104 and the first prior, Osgod, came in 1106, although the nave was not begun until 1130 and work was to last 150 years.

Siege. The Abbot of St Albans sacked Binham's prior, Thomas, but his friend Robert Fitzwalter declared himself patron and refused to accept the dismissal. The abbot laid siege to the priory in 1212, forcing the monks to starvation level and, when King John heard of the trouble and sent troops, Fitzwalter fled.

A generation later the monk Alexander de Langley drove himself mad through too much study. The prior flogged him, and ultimately buried his body in chains.

Richard de Parco, 1227–'44, was the only honourable prior. He raised a charge on Wells windmill to buy hassocks, asked another village to feed his monks when the larder was empty, did much restoration, and still had £20 when he left office. Most others could be described as crooks, with William de Somerton (1317–'35) the worst. He sold the silver and spent the money on trying to turn base metal into gold, stupid man. He was imprisoned, escaped, reinstated, then fled, leaving a debt of £600. At the dissolution in 1540 the annual income was down to £140.

Henry VIII gave the ruined priory to Thomas Paston in 1542, and the **Paston Letters** record the receipt in 1553 of 13s 7½d for rubble to build a house in Wells. Paston wanted to build himself a house here, but when falling masonry killed a labourer, his workmates saw it as an evil omen.

Restoration was in progress in 1715, and in 1809 the enormous west window opening was bricked up for safety; it had the earliest example of bar tracery in England.

Today, most outbuildings are down to ground level, leaving only the nave – but what a nave! It's an enormous parish church, and also holds a bat colony. English Heritage owns it, but there's no fee.

English Heritage also owns the damaged **Market Cross** on the green, site of the annual four-day fair from Henry I's time to the 1950s.

NORTH ELMHAM

St Augustine brought Christianity to England in 597 (don't confuse him with a namesake of 354–430) and became first Archbishop of Canterbury. St Felix – remember Babingley? – was first Bishop of East Anglia from 631, his seat at the great port of Dunwich. About 680 the region was split, roughly on the lines of North Folk and South Folk, with the northern diocese centred on Elmham. This endured until the Viking attacks and the slaughter of St Edmund in 870. Then Alfred defeated the Viking King Guthrum, who converted to Christ and made Dunwich his capital city and bishopric.

Elmham was demoted. When the See of Norfolk was reinstated, the bishop moved to Thetford in 1071 – and Dunwich gave way to Bury St Edmunds. But in 1085 the honour passed to Norwich, where it has stayed.

For ages the Elmham ruins were forgotten, called locally the 'Castle Hills.' An amateur digger in 1870 assumed they were 14th cent; in 1903 they were thought to be Saxon, and in 1962 this was proved. Finally, the ruins of Elmham came to light in 1967, with still later work dating the masonry to between 1090 and 1120. But this was *after* the bishopric moved to Thetford! In fact, the demoted cathedral was built of wood: this stone structure was North Elmham's Bishop's Chapel – with 14th cent additions as at first supposed.

Peasants' Revolt. Henry le Despenser, Bishop of Norwich in 1370, helped put down the Peasants' Revolt in 1381 and in return was given the chapel at Elmham, which he converted into a moated and fortified house. He scattered many human skeletons in the process, but his work preserved Norman masonry that would otherwise have been lost. The place was abandoned when he died in 1404, and lay forgotten until 1948. It is now under English Heritage control, open any time, free.

Church. Beside the chapel ruins is the elegant parish church, its

Signatures of more worthies with Norfolk connections: Edward VII; Queen Anne; Anne Boleyn; Charles, Viscount Townshend.

oldest part being stones in the chancel from the time of Bishop de Losinga. The chancel was in ruins by 1277 but was restored in the 15th cent. The tall tower is in three stages, and for a small fee you may climb it, for some good views. Now here's an oddity: the church (that is, the font) is dedicated to St Mary, but the south chapel is for St James and the north for St John. Such multiple dedications infer the church was important.

Elmham Park **vineyard** occupies the Saxon cemetery site and is open all year, by appointment.

BILLINGFORD. Two miles east is Billingford, site of a Roman settlement on the road from Caister to Castle Acre, and a major crossing point on the Wensum in Saxon times. The Billinga family founded the Royal House of Saxony and was prominent in the 11th cent.

FAKENHAM

Fakenham was a slow grower. It began as a 6th-cent Saxon village; it's had a market since 1250; in 1784 Messrs Gurney, Birkbeck, Buxton and Peckover established a bank on the Market Place – but it took the two railways to make the town grow.

The banking quartet didn't limit themselves to Fakenham. Gurney had a bank in Harwich; Peckover was busy in Wisbech (a descendant was co-founder of the National Trust), and in both towns he started a Quaker chapel in Quaker Lane.

Fire destroyed most of the Market Place in 1738; a bonus was the Crown Inn which replaced a hunting lodge used by John of Gaunt (Ghent), former lord of the manor.

The church of Sts Peter and Paul is probably on a Saxon site, but it was not noted in Domesday; since 1547 the patronage of the church has rested with Trinity College, Cambridge. If you find a churchwarden you may get

North Elmham Cathedral? No. It's the ruined Bishop's Chapel.

permission to climb the 146 steps in the 115ft (35m) tower. Back at ground level you may find the poor box with the date 1665; the box was lost for generations and found in 1888 in a local brewery.

The cemetery has a granite memorial to Sir George Edwards (1850–1933), magistrate, Labour MP, and founder of the National Union of Agricultural Workers.

Museum. South of town, one of the oldest gasworks in the country is now the Museum of Gas and Local History, limited opening dates. It produced gas from 1846 until the North Sea took over in 1965.

Tourist Information. Red Lion House, Market Place, 01328.851981.

The THURSFORD COLLECTION is described in detail on page 97.

PENSTHORPE WATERFOWL PARK is described in detail on page 96.

Little Snoring. Little Snoring is worth a visit, and not only for its name, which comes from a Saxon invader or settler named *Snear* – 'swift, alert;' anything but sleepy.

St Andrew's church is unique. Its round tower is Saxon, probably c1010, and it stands separate from the nave: there are freestanding *square* towers at West Walton, Beccles and Dereham. It still has its ancient dovecotes,

71

from which birds would be taken during the lean winters.

The nave, too, predates the Norman Conquest, but all else is no older than 1240. The bell was cast in 1770 and the organ was built c1880 by an amateur in Fakenham. Restored in 1987 it is now of national significance.

The nave has another surprise: four noticeboards from **R.A.F. Little Snoring**, a WW2 airfield nearby. Records of decorations begin with Sgt Rosenbloom's DFM in 1943 and end with W.O. Smith's DFC in 1945. Another board lists the enemy planes damaged or destroyed.

BALE

You're too late to see the celebrated **Bale Oak** in Bale or Bathley. It had a girth of 36ft (10.9m) at human waist level, and its longest branch stretched 75ft (23m) when the tree was felled in 1860. It was condemned to death because the parish officers refused to accept responsibility if the branches fell on anybody. The lord of the manor, Sir Willoughby–Jones, had the timber hauled to Cranmer Hall in Fakenham, in a great procession.

Somebody, somewhere, counted a thousand rings.

Stories claim that 20 people could stand inside the hollow trunk, that a cobbler made it his home, and another time that people kept pigs there. The Bale Oak is believed to be the last relic of a Celtic or Saxon sacred grove, with All Saints' Church nearby for the holy link – the only stained glass there shows oak leaves and acorns. But the nicest touch is the notice on the site:

> Here I stand all in disgrace,
> Once the wonder of this place.
> My head knocked off, my body dead,
> And all the virtue of my limbs is fled.

There's another notice in the church. It has no connection with the oak, but is interesting for its possible libellous content:

> Be it Remember'd That Thos Gay, bought of Lucy Clarke, with Bale Town Money which Sum was Sixteen Pounds Ten Shillings, A piece of Land laying in Wells…This Money was given by James Ringall to Buy Blankett to Clad the Poor of Bale, many Years Since. Anno 1774.

GODWICK, the ghost village

Five miles south of Fakenham stood Godwick. All that remains is part of a large Tudor barn now part of a modern building, and the corner of the church tower. Since the Industrial Revolution more than 200 Norfolk villages have died, but Godwick is the only one to have anything surviving.

The Saxons settled here, and Godwick survived until the Middle Ages, but a series of poor harvests on this heavy clay killed the community around 1600. Yet in 1585 Sir Edward Coke, Chief Justice to Elizabeth I and of the Holkham family, bought Godwick Manor for £3,500 and built an elegant house. He had recently married Bridget Paston, but she died in childbirth and lies in Tittleshall Church. Four months later Sir Edward married the young and wealthy widow of Sir William Hatton, but she didn't like Godwick, preferring her London home on the site of today's Hatton Garden.

The tower of Godwick's 13th-cent church, demolished soon after Coke built the hall, was left as a folly and still survives. But Godwick Hall was demolished in 1962.

The site is unfenced, but you are welcome daily Apr-Sep; park in the farmyard at the end of the approach road.

TITTLESHALL. Less than a mile across the fields, or two road miles away, is the thriving village of Tittleshall. The Church of St Mary The Virgin is unimposing from outside, yet it contains a fantasy of tombs. Here is Sir Edward Coke (see Godwick), whose memorial cost £400, and the tomb of his wife Bridget, with eight of her ten children. A long plaque lists Coke's achievements, including: Speaker of the House of Commons; Lord Chief Justice to James I; and prisoner in the Tower of London.

There's a memorial to great-grandson Robert Coke, grandfather to Coke of Norfolk, KB, Baron of Minster Lovell, Viscount of Holkham, Earl of Leicester, and builder of Holkham Hall. He was the last of the Cokes to be buried here, his funeral procession stretching 2½ miles, and the nave is overwhelmed by his magnificent memorial. His first wife Jane is remembered here, with a carving that cost a mere 3,000 guineas (£3,150) in 1805.

Mileham. Sir Edward Coke was born at Mileham in 1552. Stigand was lord of the manor here in 1043, when he became Bishop of Elmham. By 1066 he was Archbishop of Canterbury and, as such, crowned Harold who died at the Battle of Hastings. It was the Stigand link which prompted the Normans to build a castle here, but only the earthwork remains - on private land behind the village sign.

Praise to God in the parapet of Felbrigg Hall.

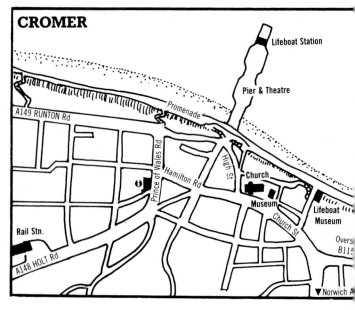

6: CROMER and AYLSHAM

Disappearing Norfolk

STAND ON THE LOW CLIFFS at Weybourne and look west. That part of the coastline is slowly extending out to sea. Now look east; that part is gradually being eroded. You are on the very spot where the two great forces of the sea meet: deposition and erosion. In fact, the cliff you are standing on is an indication of the destructive action - there are no cliffs to the west until you reach Hunstanton. West, the beaches are wide and sandy. East, they are narrow and gritty.

Weybourne Hope. You are at Weybourne Hope, where the cutting edge of the southbound tides has worn a deepish hole in the sea bed. They knew this in the 18th cent and recognised the deep water, the beach, and the undefended hinterland, as an ideal spot for invasion. Luckily, our enemies didn't know the adage:

> He who would Old England win
> Must at Weybourne Hope begin.

CROMER

The sea had claimed the church of *Shipden-juxta-Mare* by 1390, so they built another at Shipden-juxta-Felbrigg on land given by Edward III. As the area was known as Crowmere, the new community took that name.

The Church of Sts Peter and Paul was completed in Henry IV's reign, its tower at 160ft (48.7m) the tallest in Norfolk and an ideal landmark. The church prospered for a mere century until Henry VIII's actions over monasteries cut off further investment; an inventory of 1552 said that the five bells, weighing 62cwt (3,149kg) were valued at £46.10s. The decay continued: in 1681 the chancel was so dilapidated that it was demolished by gunpowder; by 1757 the nave roof had collapsed, restricting services to the base of the tower. Ten years later the Bishop of Norwich sold the brasses, and the roof lead, as well as four of the five bells. Legend claims the bells were sent by sea to their new home in St Mary le Bow Church, which would mean they became the famous **Bow Bells**, but the Whitechapel Foundry can prove that it cast the bells for St Mary le Bow and St Mary atte Bow.

Today Cromer Church has six bells weighing 2 tons 9cwt 9lb (2,493kg) – and a sign in the belfry states they are 77% copper, 23% tin.

Harry Yaxley. At the 90th of the 171 steps in the tower is an opening called Harry Yaxley's Hole. A friend held Harry's legs as he dangled outside the hole, collecting birds' eggs. The friend demanded a greater share of the yield, but Harry called back: "You shan't hev 'em."

"Then I'll drop you."

"Drop away, then," said Harry – and reached the ground quicker than he expected. He survived.

Crabs. Cromer grew slowly and was purely a fishing village until the unwanted railway began bringing tourists. As it had no harbour, all the boats were launched from the beach and hauled into town when storms threatened. The locals changed their ideas on the railway when it started carrying their crabs to a much wider market - including London.

Museums. The **Cromer Museum**, hiding behind a stone wall on Tucker St near the church, is built in fishermen's cottages of Victorian times and keeps the original cooking range and gaslamps. It tells a wonderful story of the crab fishermen, the development of Cromer as a resort, and the local geology. Open daily: 01263.513543. The **Lifeboat Museum** by the disused No 2 Lifeboat Station, is open daily May-Sep and occasionally out of season. Not surprisingly, it tells of the Cromer lifeboats, from No 1's first call-out in December 1867 to the Brixham brig *Wild Rose* No 2 was on station for a century, closing in 1967; No 1 is still in service, launched from the end of the pier.

Pier. The pier was cut in two in 1993 by a drilling rig which broke adrift in a storm, but it was back in service in 1994, as good as new. Lesser damage had been inflicted in 1953 and 1989. The **Pavilion Theatre** at the end has a reputation for attracting top-class entertainers for the summer show.

Henry Blogg. But back to the lifeboat. Henry Blogg joined the RNLI in 1894, aged 18, and retired 53 years 9 months later, in September 1947, having been the coxwain for 37 years. He won the George Cross, the BEM, the RNLI gold medal three times, the silver medal four times, the Canine Defence League silver medal – and the Queen of the Netherlands presented him with a gold watch. He died in 1954.

From 1935 to 1945 he coxed the *H F Bailey* which answered 128 calls and saved 518 lives. Peter Cadbury of the chocolate company bought the boat in 1991 and presented it to the museum as its main exhibit.

THE RESORT. Cromer is a pleasant and picturesque town, with a good shopping area, splendid gardens, and quaint backstreets around the church. The **beach** is mostly sand, with a sandcastle zone at the top, and entertainment is aimed at adults; it's not the resort for the Benidorm set. The **carnival** is in late May; for details ask the **tourist office** on Prince of Wales Rd, 01263.512497.

BEYOND CROMER: geology. The cliffs between Bacton and Weybourne show some of the best cross-sections of terminal moraines (where the glaciers ended) in the world. The layer of Weybourne Crag holds around 50 species of shells, while the several Forest Bed deposits have bones of large animals from the tropics to the sub-arctic. Some way down is the layer of **chalk**, which covers almost all of East Anglia; under Cromer it is 1,500ft (450m) thick, probably the thickest in the world.

OVERSTRAND. Overstrand – 'above the beach' – is a satellite village to the east. It has no promenade, no entertainment, and beach access is down steep paths in a cliff cut by erosion. The 14th-cent church vanished into the sea, so St Martin's is an 18th-cent replacement. The village is popular with retired people.

WEST RUNTON. Caravan and camping sites occupy some of the clifftop to the west, with others hidden among the pleasant hills formed by glacial deposits. The **beach** ranges from sand to shingle, and has a large pay car-park. Holy Trinity Church serves both East and West Runton, its 13th-cent tower being the oldest part; the nave collapsed in the 14th cent and has been rebuilt.

NORFOLK SHIRE HORSE CENTRE.

Tucked into the hills is West Runton's prime tourist attraction, the Shire Horse Centre and Countryside Collection. More details are on page 32.

SHERINGHAM

Three or more thousand years ago, early Britons were living among these rolling hills; 2,000 years ago the Romans built kilns here for firing

Wells-next-the-Sea was Wells-under-the-Sea during the 1953 East Coast Floods. The museum and tide measure are centre background.

pottery; 900 years ago Domesday mentioned a church, which was to become All Saints in Upper Sheringham.

By 1197 the Augustinian priories at Beeston Regis and **Weybourne** (both now ruined) were serving Walsingham pilgrims, but their main occupation was fishing, with boats launched from the beach. Fish merchants moved here in the 14th cent, and Sheringham was born; from 1358 it had a licence to trade with Blakeney.

Sheringham, like Cromer, never had a harbour, but it prospered nonetheless and in 1452 the church was rebuilt. Then a 16th-cent tax on all fishing boats working from Sheringham, led to detailed records being kept. So we know that in 1591 there were 22 boats, rising to a maximum of some 200, until overcrowding forced some to move to Lincolnshire. We also know that a smokehouse on Wyndham St was probably a storehouse for smugglers.

Inevitably, the town turned to boatbuilding – and that led to lifeboats. In 1838 the Hon Mrs Charlotte Upcher of Sheringham Hall gave the *Augusta*, a 33ft 16-oar boat named from her daughter. It was stored in a special building on West Cliff from 1838 to 1894, and ended its days on Ranworth Broad. The family's replacement, *Henry Ramey Upcher*, served until 1935, saving some 200 lives. It was last launched to celebrate the defeat of Japan in 1945 and now sits in its old boathouse near West Cliff.

The RNLI's old boathouse, built on Lifeboat Plain in 1867, was abandoned after storm damage, and it now holds the Sheringham Craft

Centre. The RNLI's present premises are on West Promenade, open to view in summer.

The *Augusta* is shown on the front of the **Two Lifeboats** pub on High St, the other vessel being the RNLI's *Duncan*. The pub is almost 300 years old, many of its timbers having come from wrecks. The Upcher family bought the place in 1878 as a coffee house, but it has also been a brothel and a mission-house.

Tourism. It was the coming of the railway in 1887 which changed the town's destiny. Tourists arrived. People with plenty of money came to *do nothing*, to the locals' amazement. Soon the Sheringham and the Grand hotels were built; the Mainsail Haul began attracting the famous – Vaugn Williams who worked on his *Pastoral* here; Captain Robert Falcon Scott and Sir Ernest Shackleton followed. The drinking fountain of 1814 became the town reservoir in 1862, and in 1901 a clock was added: it's today's distinctive **Clock Tower**.

In 1842 the Upchers gave the fishermen's chapel, but soon a real church was needed. In 1895 the aldermen laid the foundations of **St Peter's**, which was to cost £8,000. Strangely, it didn't become the parish church until 1953 when it was merged with Weybourne.

Zeppelin. The German airship which dropped the first bomb on Britain in WW1 chose Sheringham. The bomb went through the roof of a cottage in Whitehall Yard but never exploded. The occupier carried it away in a bucket.

Museum. Sheringham's own museum opened in 1990 in a fisherman's cottage off Station Road. Open daily in summer, weekends in winter, it has displays of fashion, fishing and local history, with a gift shop. The next cottage was the home of a washerwoman.

Lavatory. For something unusual, go to the Marble Arch (see map) for the only public toilets with stained glass windows – unless you know of any others.

THE RESORT. Sheringham is lively without being brash. The **beach** has some shingle at high tide, but sand lower down. With a few discos, video games, an amusement arcade and **Splash**, the tropical leisure pool, the town has something for every age group. Splash's hours are complex so call for details on 01263.825675.

Jet skis are permitted, subject to restrictions: call the **tourist office** on 01263.824329. The office is between the two railway stations.

The POPPY LINE

Two stations? Indeed! British Rail closed the line from here to Melton Constable in 1964. At once appeals went out: *join the M&GN Preservation Society!* Response was good but three years passed before the society could buy the three-mile section to Weybourne; by then BR had cleared the line from Melton Constable to Weybourne and was working steadily east.

The NORTH NORFOLK RAILWAY . . .

The Poppy Line has now relaid the track from Sheringham to Holt, and operates steam locos and restored rolling stock on the line, but there are diesels for standby or when there's risk of grassland fire.

In 1995 the line recommissioned the B12, an express passenger steam locomotive which hauled trains for the first time in 32 years. It came to Sheringham in 1967 after retirement from British Railways' Norwich to London run; it had been many times before, pulling the *Broadsman* or the *Norfolkman.* Restoration took years, and more than £100,000 – and the final stages were at the Malowa works in eastern Germany.

Other rolling stock. The Poppy Line already had two ex-BR locos; a J15 0-6-0 built at Stratford in 1912; a B12/3 4-6-0 of 1928; *Pony*, an 0-4-0 of 1912; and a series of 0-6-0 configurations: *Fireless*, built in 1929; *Wissington*, used by British Sugar; one from Ashington Colliery; plus *Ringshaw, Harlaxton*, and *12*, and an unnamed one from the National Coal Board.

Timetable. Up to eight trains run daily in each direction in high summer, with the season lasting Apr-Oct; there are no services Nov-Mar except the December Christmas Specials.

. . . and the EAST COAST PULLMAN

Come dine in leisure on the East Coast Pullman! On Saturday evening and Sunday lunchtimes the Pullman cars from one of the world's great trains, the *Brighton Belle*, join the North Norfolk Railway for a journey of nostalgia and elegance. Your food is prepared and cooked on the train, and served at your table as you travel at leisure from Sheringham to Holt. *Hi-de-hi* and *Dad's Army* have used the Poppy Line – you could be an extra in some future production!

Railway and dining car: phone 01263.822045. Talking timetable: 01263.825449.

●

BR pulled out of Sheringham Station in 1967 in favour of a smaller one across the main road – hence the two stations. So the enthusiasts leased the old one. Over the next 12 years they met continual opposition from a government opposed to private enterprise. They formed the North Norfolk Railway Company, raised £14,000 by sale of shares, went to a public inquiry, and finally ran their first steam train in 1976.

The high drama of steam (above), and the comedy of filming *Hi-de-hi* (below) at Weybourne.

LANGHAM GLASS

Go a little way north from Langham village centre to the flint Long Barn, built in 1722 for Langham Hall Farm. In 1981 it was converted to become the Langham Glass House, a workshop where one can see high-quality crystal glassware blown and shaped in the traditional way. The owners claim this is probably the only house in the country making glass in commercial quantities, entirely by hand. A ton of molten material is used each week, the special sand and other chemicals used in the manufacture being heated for seven and a half hours overnight at a temperature above 1,300°C.

Master glassmaker Paul Miller and designer Ronald Stennet-Wilson started the business here in 1979 with the aim of producing the finest-quality merchandise possible and, as testimony to their success, their crystal is sold world-wide.

Visitors to Langham are able to watch the process from a viewing gallery as the soft glass comes from the furnace at 1,100°C and passes from one craftsman to the next as each blends his skills. Glassware is on sale in the gift shop, with decorative paperweights, colourful animals and artistic wine glasses the favoured designs. The large visitor complex also includes a children's adventure play area, antiques and collectibles shop, bargain barn, restaurant, and a walled garden. Ample on-site parking. **Open** daily year-round; glass-making demonstrations Easter-Oct Sun-Fri; Nov-Easter Mon-Fri. 01328.830511.

Cambridge. Langham Glass has expanded into Cambridge, with a factory shop at Thompsons Lane, Quayside (01223.329144), again with demonstrations. A museum of Glass Through The Ages will have an emphasis on education. *Picture shows master glassmaker Paul Miller at work.* See also page **56**.

●

Sheringham Park. The National Trust owns Sheringham Park, a house and woodlands open daily, free on foot or a pay car-park. A boardwalk goes through rhododendrons, and there are good views, particularly of the Poppy Line. The hall is leased to a tenant; write for an appointment to see inside.

WEYBOURNE

The first military defences for Weybourne Hope were planned in 1588 with the Spanish Armada on the way. Nothing was done. Artillerymen moved in during the Napoleonic threat, but moved out afterwards.

In 1935 the Army moved in again – and stayed. Gun emplacements, trenches and barracks formed the *Weybourne Camp* anti-aircraft gunnery school. They fired at towed gliders out to sea so often that the

Sheringham fishermen complained.

Soon the camp was using catapult-launched pilotless aircraft, and experimenting with rockets. Weybourne proved vital to our defences in WW2, bringing Winston Churchill here in June 1941. Yet the Luftwaffe paid only one visit, in July 1940, when it bombed the camp and the village with no casualties. By the time the last gun was fired in October 1958 – the camp closed soon after – 250,000 troops had trained here, firing 1,500,000 shells out to sea.

Berry Savory had a military museum in Inveraray Castle, home of the dukes of Argyll, and needed to expand. When he heard that Weybourne Camp was on the market, he bought it, and in May 1988 the Duke of Argyll performed the opening ceremony of what is now

The **MUCKLEBURGH COLLECTION.** See the entry on page 33.

Weybourne Priory. The Augustinian canons came to England in the 11th cent, building their first priory in Colchester. They arrived in Weybourne by 1216 via West Acre under Sir Roger Meyngaren (now Anglicised to Mainwaring or Mannering) whose family held that manor since 1071.

The priory gained some independence in the 14th cent but was never big enough to go it alone, despite earning money from pilgrims to Walsingham. Indeed, the Bishop of Norwich noted in 1514 that there was only one canon. By 1530 the prior and cannon saw the end was nigh and sold everything in sight except for a small crucifix. The next bishop to visit found a priory that had ceased to function *without* Henry VIII's help. The empty buildings, which were collapsing, passed to Sir John Gresham, founder of Holt school, and later to the Walpole family. All that remain are stone walls 50ft (15m) high, and scars on the ground.

Church. The Austin canons absorbed the existing church into their priory and so it collapsed. For centuries the parish had neither priest nor usable church – then restoration came in 1866 and the work was completed by 1888.

Mill. The old windmill east of the village has also been restored, but it's part of a private house. A path beside it leads down to the shingle **beach**.

KELLING. A mile west lies Kelling. At the war memorial by the cross-roads is **Baron Art**, (head office at Albert St, Holt) a picture gallery housed in the old Reading Room, built in 1915. It's also a good place for second-hand books and collectables – and there's a tea-room, with convenient parking.

GRESHAM

William de Warrenne received the Gresham estates soon after the Norman Conquest. Under Henry II the village received its charter for a market, but it did not grow: maybe it was too close to Sheringham. The lack of development saved All Saints' Church so it still has its Saxon round tower.

Edmund Bacon, squire of Gresham, built a fortified manor in 1319 which became Gresham Castle, and which the Paston family bought in 1429. One Lord Moleyns besieged it when squire John was away in London, and managed to evict Mrs Paston and the servants. Soon after, the Pastons abandoned the place and now only a few ruins remain.

Gresham family. The Greshams came to prominence in the 14th cent. Two centuries later, Sir Thomas was a merchant and financial adviser to Henry VIII, Edward VI, Mary, and Elizabeth. It was he who established the **Royal Exchange** in London, which opened in 1571. But our interest is in Thomas's brother, Sir John, who moved to Holt: remember the name.

NORTH BARNINGHAM. As you leave Gresham for Holt, you may notice an isolated church at a crossroads – it's on OS grid 150372 – and find yourself in the middle of a village that has vanished.

BACONSTHORPE. The font of St Mary's Church, presented in 1886, began sinking. A search revealed a coffin under the floor, collapsing under the weight; the coffin belonged to the **Bacon** family. Now look in the centre of the roof for a shield bearing M (for Mary) and three pigs' heads. The same heads appear in stained glass in the south windows, taken from **Baconsthorpe Castle** in 1958 to repair bomb damage.

Heydon. Yet the name most prominent is Heydon, a family which had vast sheep holdings in Tudor times. Heydon's coat of arms is the engrailed cross seen on the monument blocking a window in the south aisle.

Let's digress a moment and study how the columns supporting the roof lean outward. This is a design fault as the weight of the roof is flattening the nave; there should have been sturdy buttresses outside. There aren't.

Baconsthorpe Castle. Now back to the Heydons. John of that ilk was a lawyer with a reputation for cheating, so he never applied for royal permission to fortify the house and wool-processing factory which became Baconsthorpe Castle. Family fortunes were low by 1600 and after the Civil Wars of 1642-'49 most of the castle was demolished. The gatehouse survived 200 years as Baconsthorpe Hall; the courtyard struggled on as a walled garden, but only a vestige remains. English Heritage owns it, with no restriction on entry.

Babes In The Wood. Lady Jane Grey, queen for 13 days in July 1553, was related to Thomas and Jane de Grey who were orphaned in 1562. Both were made wards of Queen Elizabeth and sent to Baconsthorpe, where they died. Their uncle claimed their inheritances – £300 a year for Thomas, £500 cash for Jane. Bad luck struck the uncle and he soon died.

That's the true story, and it's the basis for the story of the Babes In The Wood.

Gresham's School in Holt has grown enormously since 1900.

HOLT and GRESHAM'S SCHOOL

When Sir John Gresham (remember him?) arrived in Holt in 1546, he bought the Manor House for £170 and converted it into a school for the sole purpose of teaching boys grammar: a 'grammar school.' He endowed the school with land in 12 parishes, and houses in Cripplegate, London. In October 1556 he appointed the 'Wardens of the Mistery of Fishmongers' as governors, and a week later he died of the plague.

The school opened in 1562 for 30 scholarship boys, plus fee-payers. Almost all teachers were ordained churchmen who needed a licence from the bishop, who therefore controlled the curriculum, and made 'visitations' to check it.

Cambridge. Thomas Tallis, headmaster in 1606, made Gresham's school one of the best in the region, sending 24 boys to Caius College, Cambridge, during his 34 years in office. And he left his private library to the school.

A Royalist uprising in Holt in 1650, the year after Charles I lost his head, showed mass opposition to Cromwell. On Christmas Day 25 Royalists were executed at Norwich, including Thomas Cooper, an usher at the school, but local legend claims he was headmaster and was hanged at the school.

Fire. Timber and thatch houses have always been a fire risk. On Mayday 1708 most of the town burned down, causing damage worth £20,000; the fire travelled so fast, it was said, that nobody could save the meat from the market stalls. The thatched chancel of the church blazed, and molten lead from the nave burned holes in the stone floor – the signs are still there. Gresam's school escaped with minor damage, and the rebuilt town moved a little to the west.

In 1729 John Holmes was appointed headmaster. Holmes, who was *not* a churchman, added geography and history, and when he didn't like existing textbooks, he wrote his own. The next head was a preacher, and became vicar of Sheringham and Weybourne while still ruling the school. The divided loyalty showed; two rival schools opened in Holt, taking most of his pupils. A new lay head had to work hard, adding arithmetic, geometry, Latin and Greek – but his successors were still churchmen.

Then came Mr Howson. Given the headship in 1900, in 19 years he transformed a lacklustre local school with 44 boys into a public school of national appeal. He added science, French and German; he abolished the cane; he had new buildings, the nucleus of the present school. But most of all, he turned the institution into Gresham's *School*, without alienating the people of Holt who wanted it to keep its local character.

By 1988 Sir John Gresham's school was charging £7,275 a year each for 470 senior boarders (plus 200 at prep) and employing a staff of 225 who were paid £2,000,000 a year. In many respects, Gresham's School *is* Holt.

St Andrew's Church. The fire destroyed much of interest in the town, but the church suffered only roof damage. Memorials include those to John Holmes and Thomas Cooper from the school; and William Briggs, physician to William III. But the church is unusual in that pipistrelle bats breed in the nave, jackdaws nest in the tower, and the churchyard is a nature reserve.

The modern town has plenty of character in its mock-old buildings and winding alleys: Picturecraft has an art gallery in Lee's Courtyard (01263.713259), and there's a small *museum* nearby. And Baron Art is in Albert St (01263.713906).

LETHERINGSETT

Early in the 20th cent a blacksmith wrote this bill:

The bill:		The translation:
Osforarfada	2/–	Horse for half a day
Afortheos	1/–	Hay for the horse
Ashuinonim	2/–	A-shoeing of him
Anafechinonimagin	1/–	And a-fetching of him again

Water mill. The Domesday record mentions 'Leringaseta;' in 1384 other records tell of John de Keyly and William de Gatele buying 48 acres *and a watermill*. By 1720 John Brereton owned the mill, the house which became Letheringsett Hall, and a brewery. The mill burned down but was rebuilt by 1754; it burned again in 1800 and was again rebuilt. The supply of water to the millpond had been agreed in 1765, but in 1945 a diesel engine replaced waterpower. Too late. The public now wanted powder-fine white flower, so the mill closed.

Restoration began in 1982 using the original water-wheel, and Lether-ingsett Mill is again in business, claiming to be Norfolk's only working water-mill. It produces 2.5 tons of flour a week, most sold on the premises for animal and pet food. It's *open* select afternoons in summer.

St Andrew's. The round tower of the church was built after Domesday, but is pure Saxon in style, with 15th-cent windows. In 1236 a local man had given land to Binham Priory which, in return, built the rest of the church; the prior of Binham appointed priests from 1308 to 1422.

In 1786 John Burrell, son-in-law of Mr Holmes, Gresham's headmaster, was rector, giving free reign to his love of insects. Burrell sold most of the estate to William Hardy who was mad on trees and (as his epitaph states) *clothed these once-barren hills with foliage.* And probably helped feed Burrell's insects. Keble College, Oxford, now holds the patronage.

Johnson Jex. Look at the tombstone just inside the churchyard. Johnson Jex taught himself the art of watchmaking, but first had to teach himself French in order to read a book on the subject. He made every tool he needed, and even engraved this inside a watch he made:

> I, Johnson Jex, a blacksmith bred,
> With some strange crankums in my head
> And tools on which I could depend
> By me invented. For a friend
> This time-piece made from end to end.
> If this your mind it should perplex
> Behold my name, 'tis Johnson Jex. ⌐

Bayfield. Bayfield is another vanishing village. There's only the Hall, and the ivy-clad skeleton of the church, which was abandoned in 1927. Its last patron was none other than Sir Alfred Joddrell who built Glandford Church.

FELBRIGG HALL

The Felbrigg family built the first Felbrigg Hall, but the present beautiful mansion is the work of the Windham family and was begun in 1620. William Windham I planted the chestnuts in the 600-acre 240ha) park, but it was Wm Windham II who worked on the hall from 1741, after his Grand Tour. He decorated the interior, extended the place to house his paintings from the tour – they're still there and are a major feature. And it was he who added the mirrors, damask and furniture in the main rooms.

William Windham III, 'Weathercock Windham' (he knew which way the political wind blew), added the final touches. But it was 'Mad' Windham who went broke in 1863 and had to sell Felbrigg, John Ketton being the buyer. His grandson gave the hall to the National Trust in 1970 and its now **open** Apr-Oct most days.

Gloria Deo. Main enlargements were in 1674–'87 and in 1750, giving the house a Jacobean style with some excellent stucco. The imposing south front, framed by three chimney stacks, has the words GLORIA DEO IN EXCELSIS set in the stonework of the parapet.

The hall has a restaurant and shop open Apr-Xmas, and the park is open daily, year round, dawn to dusk, thus allowing access to the parish **Church of St Margaret**, with its monuments to the Felbrigg and Windham families. There are brasses dating from 1351, and work by Grinling Gibbons.

CHURCHES and CRAFTS

South from Felbrigg, there's Andrew and Joanna Young's **Pottery** at Lower Gresham, who have samples of their stoneware in the Victoria and Albert Museum. Open all year, 01263.577548.

Ancient St Mary the Virgin at **Roughton** has a short Saxon tower. **Thurgarton**'s thatched All Saints' had a Saxon tower until its collapse in 1882, but St Mary's at **Aldborough** has Saxon puddingstone masonry in the nave. Neither church has a tower. **Thwaite**'s round tower is Norman; St Ethelbert's at **Alby** has Saxon remains but the main interest is the rood stairs.

In the village, call at **Alby Crafts** on the crossroads. Valerie Alston (01263.761590) has restored farm buildings to hold studios producing a range of crafts in textiles, pottery, woodwork, graphic art, and others: they change from time to time. There's also a **Lace Museum** and a **Bottle Museum**, claimed to be unique in Britain. Open Mar-Dec Tues-Sun.

Our Lady and St Margaret's at **Calthorpe** has a north-facing Devil's door, and a corbel with two female faces, one of them gagged. **Erpingham**'s Church of St Mary has a tall tower, and a font rescued from St Benedict's in Norwich, a victim of WW2 bombs. See the brass of Sir John de Erpingham whose son Thomas built the Erpingham Gate at Norwich Cathedral.

St Lawrence's at **Ingworth** lost its Saxon round tower in 1822 so the stump is thatched to match the nave roof.

WOLTERTON and MANNINGTON

Wolterton Hall, west of Calthorpe, was built for Horace Walpole between 1727 and 1741. It was abandoned in 1858 in favour of Mannington Hall, which was badly damaged by fire in 1952. Following the death of the owner, Lord Walpole, in 1989, the heir began major restoration to reopen Wolterton. Guided tours to parts of the house are available by appointment, and there are walks in the grounds. Both grounds are open in summer; for details call 01263.584175.

Wolterton Hall holds the **Hawk and Owl Trust**, active in conservation but not rescue; open from Easter.

AYLSHAM

This small market town has an unspoiled centre based on the Buttlands, where townsmen were obliged to practise archery until the 18th cent; it's now a car park. Look for the charming Black Boy Inn in Queen Anne style, the 17th-cent Manor House, Old Hall and The Knoll.

The town was first recorded around the Norman Conquest when Brithric was the Saxon priest. From 1087 Battle Abbey appointed the priest and collected the tithes, but Henry VIII sent the tithes to Canterbury after he sacked Battle.

Aylsham was a prominent wool and linen town: in 1327 Edward II bought 3,500 ells (1 ell = 45in = 114cm) of 'Aylleshamme.' John of Gaunt, father of Henry IV, became squire of Aylsham in 1372, making it the main town in Norfolk of the Duchy of Lancaster. When Gaunt died in 1399, Sir Thomas Erpingham became lord of the manor and influenced affairs of St Michael's Church.

Legend claims Edward III chose the church site, but the Victorian influence is strong, as the old box pews remain, looking like an old-style railway carriage. But come here any Monday lunchtime May-Oct for a concert.

Humphry Repton. Probably the best-known resident in the cemetery is Humphry Repton, the landscape gardener who was second only to Capability Brown; he died in 1818.

Under Queen Mary when England again saw the Pope as the head of the Church, John Bury, Vicar of Aylsham, condemned glove-maker Thomas Hudson as a heretic and had him burned at the stake in Norwich.

Felbrigg Hall is a beautiful home in Jacobean style.

Bury is mentioned in Fox's *Book of Martyrs* as *a very evil man . . . a great swearer, given to women, persecuting the gospel and compelling men to idolatry*.

Black Sheep. Mrs Clare Hoare swapped a lawn mower for six black Welsh Mountain sheep in 1966. She keeps their 1,000 descendants at Ingworth where the fleece is harvested to supply the knitwear factory of Black Sheep Ltd in Penfold St, Aylsham.

BURE VALLEY RAILWAY

Would you like to drive a steam train? The one-third-scale Bure Valley Railway offers two-day courses in this boyhood dream – or you can just be a passenger on the nine-mile route between Aylsham and Wroxham; there's ample parking at each station.

The railway opened in 1991 on the old Great Eastern trackbed and offers a fascinating 45-minute run in either direction (or each direction if you want a return trip), with 30 minutes in turnaround time. You can make a full-day excursion by reserving your seat; the miniature coaches are enclosed. There's a restaurant, baby-changing room and tourist centre at Aylsham, and gift shops at both ends. 01263.733858 for timetables.

BLICKLING HALL

Beautiful Blickling is one of the top four stately homes of Norfolk, and is the regional home of the National Trust, its owner.

Anne Boleyn. Blickling is well-known as the birthplace of Anne Boleyn, but it wasn't in this house: she arrived in 1507, 109 years before the hall was built. Harold owned the Blicking lands until 1066, but William the Conqueror gave them to Bishop Losinga of Norwich, from whom they passed to the Fastolf family; Shakespeare turned a later Fastolf into his comic character Falstaff.

Thomas, Earl of Wiltshire, was the father of Anne and George Boleyn. Anne was too beautiful for safety, distracting Henry VIII even while he was wed to Catherine of Aragon. When the Spanish queen could not produce sons who survived infancy (see Walsingham), Henry married Anne, some say in November 1552, others claiming January 1553 – but Henry was married to Catherine until May 1553. Anne gave birth to the future Elizabeth I in September '53 and lost her head on the block on 19 May 1536, two days after her brother George. This line of the family expired, but the name survives as 'Bullen.' Some say that Anne herself survives, in the form of a ghost who haunts the hall.

Modern Blickling. Sir Henry Hobart, Lord Chief Justice, began rebuilding Blickling in 1616, his son completing the work. The hall passed to the Marquess of Lothian, and the 11th marquess was Britain's ambassador to the USA when he died in 1940, leaving the hall and the 4,500 acre (1,800ha) estate to the National Trust. The hall is **open** Apr-Oct daily (not

The deserted village of Godwick. All that remains is part of the church tower.

Mon, Thur) afternoons; for details call 01263.733084.

Main attractions are the front lawns, the rear gardens part designed by Humphry Repton, the Long Gallery built by the 2nd Earl of Buckingham to hold a tapestry of Peter the Great, the enormous library, and George II's bedhangings in the state bedroom.

St Andrew's. Blicking's stubby-towered church is mainly 15th cent but has numerous brasses – there's one to Nicholas de Dagworth, builder of the first hall; to Anna Boleyn who died in 1479; to Roger and Cecily Felthorp with their 10 sons and 6 daughters; and others.

The COAST to HAPPISBURGH

Down the A149, **Thorpe Market** has a towerless church built in 1795–'96 in mock Gothic, but **Southrepps** has a traditional church with a tower 114ft (34.5m) high and was as big as a cathedral before it lost its aisles in 1791. **Trimingham** has its Church of St John the Baptist's Head, a bizarre dedication supporting belief that the severed head was actually here. People even came on pilgrimage to see it.

William de Warrenne was lord of the manor of **Gimingham** as well as founder of the Cluniac Priory at Lewes, Sussex, which still appoints the parsons here. The thatched Church of St Nicholas at **Swafield** shows the saint with his three bags of gold. **Trunch**'s Church of St Botolph survived the Puritanic purge of 1643 because the chancel was used as a school-room; see the initials scratched on the walls. **Knapton** has one of England's best double-hammerbeam roofs, made from Irish oak in 1503.

Legend claims it was cargo in a wrecked ship. **Antingham** is an oddity; the ruins of the 12th-cent church are beside the still-used St Mary's. The brass to Richard Calthorpe shows him with his 19 children.

WORSTEAD. This tiny village was so important in medieval times that it gave its name to a type of cloth. The village is a collection of pleasant houses around a market square. **Geoffrey the Dyer's House** is named from Geoffrey Litester who led the local Peasants' Revolt against the Poll Tax. Yet he never lived in this house!

St Mary's. The church, begun in 1379, is big enough to hold the entire parish several times over, a testimony to the age of wool. The tower is 109ft (33m) tall but, inside, you are awed by the vast size, the box pews and the hammerbeam roof. St Mary's Guild of Weavers, Spinners and Dyers keeps a **museum** of the days of glory, showing wool samples and how to weave the material which is still popular for men's suits.

MUNDESLEY. William Cowper spent his last years (1795–1800) between Mundesley and East Dereham. Cowper, best known for his poem *John Gilpin*, was suffering from depression and eventually quit Mundesley because he didn't like the east wind.

The village, pronounced 'Munzly,' was called Muleslai in Domesday, and made its living from fishing. The railway's arrival in 1898 brought tourists, who still come despite the railway's departure in 1964. The Royal Hotel claims that Horatio Nelson stayed there while he studied at North Walsham.

It had a lifeboat from 1811 to 1895; under its cox William Withers the boat saved six men on 17 November 1868 then went out the next day and saved the entire crew from another ship. In the 19th cent small boats would be beached on the top of the tide, discharge their cargo of coal into horse-drawn carts, load up with grain, and be away on the next flood tide.

Mundesley sits on a vein of clay which provided material for most of its bricks, but the last trace of the industry is the office at the Kiln Cliffs Caravan Park: it's an old kiln.

All Saints' Church, a towerless modern renovation of a 14th-cent ruin, had two notorious rectors in Tudor times. John Russell was a part-time poacher, and James Matchett was a minor criminal often in court.

Stow Mill. South of the village is Stow Mill, built in 1827 and abandoned in the 1930s. Mike Newton bought it in 1971 and has done most of the restoration. It's open daily, usually unattended, so leave your donation in the box.

Mundesley today. The village offers quiet beach holidays; the sands are moderately wide and accommodation ranges from smart hotel to caravan site. **Tourist office:** Station Rd, 01263.721070.

PASTON and BACTON. The tiny village of Paston owes its fame to the Paston family who corresponded with the leaders of society from 1422 to 1509. The **Paston Letters** are among the earliest surviving texts in English, and offer an insight into life in those times.

High tide on the coast of Norfolk; sheltered boating at Blakeney Creek.

The Pastons kept the letters as a family record, but when the last in line, William Paston, Earl of Yarmouth, died in 1732, the records were sold. A Diss chemist bought them, sold them on to John Fenn of East Dereham, who published them in stages. This letter was written in 1425, the þ an early form of *th* as in 'the.'

> To my well beloued John Staynford of Furnyvales Inne.
> To enquerre and wyte whether þe stoon may be sawed or nought, and whether it wille chippe or chynne or affraye with frost of weder or water.
> Al-so þat euery pece of þe stoon be iij foote longe and þat xv tunne tygh…[lost]…of þe stoon be euery weel bedded in-to þe walle and a foote thikke þat it ryse in heighte a foote in þe walle..

Difficult, isn't it? In 1464 the first John Paston petitioned Edward IV to urge him to make certain appointments to the church:

> To the Kyng owre sovereyn Lord
> Please it yowre Highnes to graunte vn-to yowre humble seruant John Paston the older, squier, yowr gracious lettres patentz of licence to fownde, stabilysh, and endewe in the gret mancion of Castre be Mekyll Yermowth [Caister by Great Yarmouth; *muckle* is a dialect word still in use, meaning 'much' or 'great'] in Norffolk, that late was John Fastolffes, knyght, cosyn to yowre seyd besecher, a colage of vij prystes…

There are numerous mentions of the Pastons in the thatched church of St Margaret, but the most imposing monument is the large **Paston Barn** built in 1581 in a neighbouring field. This is a tourist attraction yet to be exploited.

North Sea Gas. East of the barn we return to modern times with the **Bacton Gas Terminal**. The Dutch struck methane two miles down in 1959, and Britain found its own reserves in 1965 in the West Sole field, piped ashore in Holderness. But our biggest fields – Leman, Hewett, Dottie Deborah and others – lay off Norfolk. The receiving terminal you see here behind wire fences, covers 200 acres (80ha) and can handle 4,000,000,000cu ft (115,000,000 cu m) a day. You could drive by and not notice it.

Bromholm Priory. South of Bacton are the ruins of Bromholm Priory which, despite their history, are not worth seeing.

HAPPISBURGH. The Domesday survey called this village Hapes-burgh but the locals now call it *Hayz-br*. William the Conqueror gave the manor to Roger Bigod, of the family which produced the dukes of Norfolk, but when William d'Albini, head of the royal household, married Bigod's daughter Maud, he received Happisburgh as a dowry.

Bishop Bonner's Cottage Museum with Dereham's parish church in the background.

Albini built Castle Rising, founded a priory which was to become Wymondham Abbey, and gave Happisburgh to the priory's first abbot.

Dangerous coast. In the 14th cent the Norman church was demolished to make way for the present structure, its tower to serve as a landmark for 500 years along a dangerous stretch of coast, for the Happisburgh Sands are not far offshore.

Daniel Defoe, author of **Robinson Crusoe**, commented in 1724 on the number of ships' timbers used in barns and houses. Despite the tower helping navigators, the churchyard holds hundreds of shipwreck victims, including a mass grave for 119 seamen from HMS *Invincible*, proved to be vincible in March 1801.

Lighthouses. Two lighthouses were here when the warship went down; one was demolished late in the 19th cent. When Trinity House announced in June 1988 that it wanted to decommission the remaining light, local people objected. Within a month the Happisburgh Lighthouse Trust was formed, but it learned that only Trinity House may operate a lighthouse. The NatWest Bank paid the £15,000 that was needed to get a new Act through Parliament, and in August 1990 the trust began running Britain's only private working light. It's not open to the public.

Church. The Rev Thomas Lloyd noted in 1793 there were very few baptisms in Happisburgh. Suspecting that people couldn't afford the customary party afterwards, he offered mass baptism with a free feast to follow – and 170 people came.

7: SWAFFHAM and DEREHAM

High Norfolk

THE ANCIENT market towns of Swaffham and East Dereham (West Dereham is near Downham Market) grew because they were on the coaching road to Norwich, now the A47. But, as Norfolk was bypassed by the Industrial Revolution, their growth was restricted – and therein lies their charm.

SWAFFHAM

As you enter the market place from the west you cannot miss the town sign showing the Swaffham Pedlar 'who by a dream did find great fortune.'

Legend claims that the pedlar, John Chapman, dreamed if he went to London Bridge he would meet a man who would make his fortune. When he arrived, a man asked why he was loitering, so Chapman told of his dream. The Londoner scoffed, saying if *he* paid attention to dreams he would have gone to Swaffham and dug in the garden of a man called Chapman. The pedlar went home and unearthed a pot full of gold coins with another pot, twice as big, beneath it.

The real Chapman. The truth is that John Chapman was a merchant and churchwarden, who helped finance the building of the church around 1460; there are several carvings of him and his dog around the building.

CASTLE ACRE

North of Swaffham is the sleepy village of Castle Acre, overwhelmed by the impressive ruins of the 12th-cent church of a Cluniac Priory. Little remains of the vast priory, but the west front of the church has survived very well. The prior's lodgings still have part of the roof in place and hint at sumptuous living. The castle itself began life as a Norman manor house, later fortified, and is on a separate site in the village with enough masonry left to give an indication of what was here.

The ivy-clad bailey gate, in the centre of the village, is the oldest arch-way in Norfolk through which modern traffic may pass. All is now owned by English Heritage and is open year round.

PENSTHORPE WATERFOWL PARK

The park, occupying a 200-acre (80ha) site on the banks of the River Wensum, offers a day out with a difference for the entire family. The park has wetland reserves, woodland, meadow, and there are lakeside nature trails to explore.

More than 100 species of exotic and endangered waterfowl can be seen here, either in the lakes or in walk-through enclosures; they include king eiders from the Arctic, red-breasted geese from Siberia and pygmy geese from the tropics. In the wader enclosures there are avocets and ruffs, while scarlet ibis and bald ibis are free-flying in their own enclosure.

Work began on landscaping the reserve in 1982, after 1,000,000 tons of gravel were excavated in five years. A bird-ringing station was established in that first season, and ringing is still carried on, providing information on the habits of migratory birds such as widgeon.

Pensthorpe covers a wide range of habitats, including woodland and ancient water meadows; the woodland is home to many species of birds including long-tailed tits, nuthatch and tree creepers. Plant species include bluebell, campion, marsh-marigold and the rare marsh orchid; lesser creatures include butterflies and dragonflies, shrews and stoats, and many more.

The **Wetland World Education Centre** has a video explaining the three nature trails, plus brass engravings of birds suitable for making rubbings, and microscopes for examining feathers; schools are particularly welcome and educational materials are available in the shop. In 1994 the park won the BT *Countryside For All* regional award.

A new feature is the courtyard gallery, featuring photographic, art and craft exhibits with a wildlife theme, open year round; a new video shows the threats facing the North Sea and its fragile ecology.

The Courtyard Restaurant offers home-cooked food; there's also a gift-shop and a children's adventure play area.

Open weekends Jan-Mar; daily Apr-Dec, 1100-1700. Ample parking; facilities for disabled. 01328.851465. *Picture shows children feeding black-necked swans from South America.* See also page 71.

●

DEREHAM

Dereham's legends are about the town's creator, Withburga, youngest daughter of King Anna who established a convent here in 654. Withburga found she was running short of food so the Virgin Mary sent two wild deer each day for her to milk and so save the community. When death called, she was buried in a tomb over which a chapel was built, and for centuries this tomb drew pilgrims to Dereham.

Withburga's sister Ethelreda had begun her own convent at Ely, but in 974 the monks decided that Withburga's remains should rest in Ely, not

Dereham. They threw a banquet in Dereham and stole the body by night; legend claims the body was in perfect condition. The Virgin Mary compensated Dereham by making a spring of clear water flow from the open tomb, which brought even more pilgrims.

St Withburga's spring dried up in the 18th cent but her open tomb is still visible amid the ruins of the chapel behind St Nicholas's Church. St Nicholas? Why wasn't it St Withburga's?

The church has two towers. As the original is not sturdy enough to hold the eight bells, a freestanding tower was added in1530. This later tower was used as a prison for French trooper Jean de Narde during the Napoleonic Wars. Narde escaped, was shot, and is buried near St Withburga's tomb. And the churchtower is now the **tourist office**, open Apr-Sep.

Bishop Bonner. Near the churchyard entrance is **Bishop Bonner's Cottage Museum**, in one of the quaintest buildings surviving in East Anglia. Edward Bonner was the local rector from 1534 to '38 before becoming Bishop of London. The three cottages, knocked into one, have the date MDII (1502) in the pargeting, but the Bonner link is unknown. Part

●

The THURSFORD COLLECTION

Young George Cushing went from Thursford to King's Lynn in 1920 to see the fair. He was so spellbound at the music, lights and steam engines that, a few years later, he bought a second-hand steam engine and hired it out. He kept buying them, especially when petrol ousted steam and the traction engines were selling at scrap value.

More years passed. Steam engines became a novelty and their price soared. George started steam rallies and the crowds came pouring in. Eventually his bizarre fleet became the Thursford Collection, based in the farm where he stored those early machines. In 1977 the collection became a charitable trust for the preservation of steam, and added fairground attractions, such as Wurlitzer and other organs, static steam engines, and a fairground carousel.

Christmas carols. When the Wurlitzer came in 1976 from the Paramount Cinema in Leeds, it needed a special building to house it, as the roundabout did two years later. Reginald Dixon, who played another Wurlitzer at the Tower Ballroom, Blackpool, came to play at Thursford, but now a resident organist gives concerts every afternoon in the season, as well as at the Christmas carol concerts which began in 1977 and attract 50,000 people a year – and were seen on national television in 1991.

Open. The collection is at Thursford Green, near Fakenham, and is open daily Apr-Oct, and around Christmas. 01328.878477. *Picture shows an enormous 112-key Mortier dance organ. See also page 71.*

of the building became a museum in 1963, the rest added in 1968 to make a museum of local history and literati, but the building itself is the main exhibit; one passage is so narrow that visitors walk sideways. Open May-Sep Tues-Sat afternoons.

Borrow and Cooper. William Cowper, not liking the east wind at Mundesley, moved to a house by Dereham Market Place where the Congregational Church now stands, and spent four miserable years here. His remains lie in St Nicholas's churchyard.

By contrast, George Borrow's parents were married in the church, Borrow was brought up here, but his mother went to Dumpling Green, a mile south, for the birth. Borrow is best known for his *Lavengro*, published in 1851.

GRESSENHALL MUSEUM

In 1774 Dereham burghers built an enormous workhouse for 700 luckless people; today it is the splendid Gressenhall Museum. It's on the B1146 north-east of town, open Easter-Oct Tues-Sun; 01362.860563.

The museum holds a wide range of photos and artefacts showing rural life in the past 150 years, with other sections recalling the tools of now defunct trades. The largest display is, understandably, of farm implements – from seed drills similar to Jethro Tull's, to a threshing machine built by William Foster of Lincoln, who built the first Army tank.

Visit the seedsman's shop, the dairy, the forge, the weaver's shop, the saddlery, and the country cottage. And keep an eye open for the *mawkin* – that's what Norfolk folk used to call a scarecrow.

Some of the splendid exhibits at Gressenhall Museum near Dereham.

KINGS and QUEENS of ENGLAND

from 1066 to 1901

1066–1087 **William I,** William the Conqueror, first of the Norman kings. At the end of his reign the Domesday Book is compiled, listing everything of value in the land.

1087–1100 **William II,** William Rufus.

1100–1135 **Henry I,** The Lion of Justice, younger brother of William II Dies in Normandy.

1135–1154 **Stephen.**

1154–1189 **Henry II,** who rules most of the British Isles and half of France. Feudalism dies at the start of his reign.

1189–1199 **Richard I,** Richard the Lion-Heart or *Coeur de Lion,* goes on crusades and spends only months in England.

1199–1216 **John,** called 'Lackland' because he loses much of the French territory.

1216–1272 **Henry III,** crowned at the age of 10. In his reign Magna Carta becomes recognised as the law of the land.

1272–1307 **Edward I,** in whose reign wool becomes of major economic importance, particularly in East Anglia.

1307–1327 **Edward II,** elder son of Edward I. He is deposed in favour of his son and allegedly murdered with a red-hot poker in the anus.

1327–1377 **Edward III.** The French liaison is breaking down and in 1338 the Hundred Years War begins against France. The Black Death strikes in 1348. By 1375 England has lost all but a few towns in France.

1377–1399 **Richard II.** The first experiment with the poll tax results in the Peasants' Revolt of 1381.

1399–1413 **Henry IV,** with a weak claim to the throne, survives several battles but dies of an epileptic fit.

1413–1422 **Henry V,** who recovers some of the French provinces, dies from dysentery at Vincennes, aged 36.

1422–1461 **Henry VI** becomes king at the age of eight months. After Joan of Arc is burned at the stake the Earl of Suffolk proposes Henry marry Margaret of Anjou. In 1453 the king goes mad, shortly before the Wars of the Roses.

1461–1483 **Edward IV** succeeds from the deposed Henry while Lancaster and York continue to fight. Edward dies from pneumonia, aged 40.

1483 **Edward V** reigns from 9 April to 25 June but is victim of intrigue and dies, one of the 'princes in the Tower.'

1483–1485 **Richard III,** Edward's uncle, seizes the throne but dies at the Battle of Bosworth.

1485–1509 **Henry VII** brings in the Tudor dynasty and invades France yet again, while Columbus discovers America.

1509–1547 **Henry VIII,** the most outrageous king on the English throne, takes six wives. Because the Pope refuses to acknowledge divorce Henry breaks from the Catholic Church and Protestantism begins. Cardinal Wolsey of Ipswich is for a while the power behind the throne. Henry dies, aged 55, from problems with his leg.

1547–1553 **Edward VI,** Henry's only son becomes king. The peasants revolt again in Norfolk in 1549, and Edward dies of tuberculosis, aged 15.

1553 **Lady Jane Gray** is proclaimed queen on 6 July but loses her support on the 19th; she loses her head the next year.

1553–1558 **Mary I** becomes queen while staying at Framlingham Castle, Suffolk. She marries Philip of Spain who claims the English throne – unsuccessfully. Mary dies from flu.

1558–1603 **Elizabeth I ,** Good Queen Bess, is probably England's most charismatic queen. In her reign Drake sails around the world and later defeats the Spanish Armada.

1603–1625 **James I,** who is James VI of Scotland, unites the two kingdoms. Guy Fawkes tries to blow up Parliament.

1625–1649 **Charles I.** Charles dismisses Parliament in 1629, but it grows strong and in 1642 the Civil War starts, Parliament versus the Crown. Charles is publicly beheaded at Whitehall and the Monarchy falls.

1649–1660 **The Commonwealth.** Oliver Cromwell becomes Lord Protector.

1660–1685 **Charles II,** son of the last king, regains the throne. The Plague strikes in 1665 and the Great Fire of London destroys the city in 1666. Charles dies of apoplexy, having secretly received the last rites of the Catholic Church.

1685–1689 **James II** encourages Catholicism but is overthrown by a Protestant revolution.

1689–1702 **William III and Mary II** are offered the throne, but a Protestant succession is demanded. Mary dies from smallpox in 1694 and William rules alone.

1702–1714 **Anne,** daughter of James II, satisfies the legal requirement and so reigns. The 1707 Act of Union legally binds England and Scotland.

1714–1727 **George I** ushers in the House of Hanover. Sir Robert Walpole creates the post of Prime Minister. George has a heart attack near Osnabrück, aged 67.

1727–1760 **George II.** Britain expands into North America and India.

1760–1820 **George III,** the longest-reigning king.

1820–1830 **George IV.** An unpopular monarch, George dies of liver failure after too much drinking.

1830–1837 **William IV** dies from the same cause, aged 71.

1837–1901 **Victoria,** grand-daughter of George III, is the longest-reigning monarch of all, coming to the throne aged 18.

And more royal signatures: Richard II (Le Roy R2); Henry IV (HR); Henry V (RH); James I; Charles I; Edward V (R. Edwardus Quintus).

INDEX